Silly Su

Judy Moore

S.B. Publications

Contents

Published by
S B Publications
19 Grove Road
Seaford
East Sussex BN25 1TP
01323 893498
sbpublications@tiscali.co.uk

©Jem Editorial 2004
ISBN 1-85770-294-8

Designed and typeset by
Jem Editorial

Printed by
Fotolito Lungo, Italy

Cover picture:
Boundary fence at
St Peter's School, Chailey

Preface

This county, the land of the South Saxons, was once known as Silly Sussex – perhaps, to furriners from the sheeres, it still is. We in Sussex maintain that 'silly' comes from the Saxon *saelig* or *soelig*, a word meaning holy, blessed, innocent or good, and that our county, and we, were so-called because of the many churches and good Christian inhabitants here. Which is why the Devil wanted to drown Sussex by cutting a great dyke through the Downs from the sea. A silly story if ever I heard one.

Silly can mean foolish, witless, stupid, weak, impotent, helpless, harmless, guileless, frail and inoffensive. But *saelig/soelig* also meant happy, prosperous and fortunate. Detractors claimed that the silly in Silly Sussex was earned 'on account of the stupidity of the natives', a slander it was sometimes difficult to refute when the loony utterances of eccentrics and rural 'characters' were bruited about by patronising toffs as examples of sparkling Sussex wit. *Viz*, as they used to say:

> An old fellow who used very often to visit my father was one day standing near the oast houses at the farm in Battle and he appeared to be admiring the view. Suddenly, however, he amused my father by saying: 'I reckon, Will, if there was an east wind a-blowing, and you stood here naked, with a wet sack round your shoulders, eating a cold bullace pie without any sugar, you wouldn't be very hot.'

While we may well be holy, innocent, inoffensive, good, witless and so on, we can be pretty silly (as in daft) too. Witness Bonfire as celebrated in Lewes where, instead of the Fifth being along the lines of a carnival, with floats and fun-fair as elsewhere in Sussex, the occasion is deadly serious. Massed Lewesians parade the streets in spangly costumes and furry off-cuts. They blow up truck-sized effigies of popes, politicians and 'public enemies' – but they never crack a smile. Seven or so hours of brilliant pyrotechnics would, you'd think, be fun stuff. Not for the bonfire boys. 'We're doing it in remembrance of the Protestant Martyrs'; 'We're commemorating the failure of the Gunpowder Plot' they say, resolutely po-faced, as is *de rigueur* in Lewes on the Fifth.

Ford Madox Heuffer (as Kent man Ford Madox Ford used to be called) declared it was the incorporation of Pevensey and Seaford into the Cinque Ports in the sixteenth century that established the county's reputation for stupidity. He could have been right.

A gloriously silly story, that may well be apocryphal as no evidence exists, concerns the official opening of Wealden District Council's headquarters at Crowborough in April 1988 by the Marquis of Abergavenny. It's said that incised on a lintel was a Latin phrase translating as 'welcome all who enter here', which amused a medical doctor at the ceremony who read the Latin as 'welcome all who enter these *female private parts*'. Council officers say it never happened, and nobody now admits to seeing the legend which, allegedly, was swiftly removed.

Silly may also mean amusing, funny, humorous, bizarre and eccentric, which is not a bad description of those of us who dwell in Sussex by the sea. Here, to entertain you, are a few amusing daftnesses and little sillinesses from across the centuries. **JEM**

Concerned in liquor

The *Sussex Weekly Advertiser* of August 25, 1794, carried this report:

Last Wednesday morning Messrs. Lindsey and Geere, riding officers at Rottingdene, seized 51 tugs of Geneva which they found concealed in a cavern at Telscombe, made by the smugglers for that purpose. The officers plugged one tub and invited all the old women of the Parish to partake of it, which they helped to drink out, and some of them had sipped so largely of the enlivening extract that they soon found themselves stimulated, as if under the provoking influence of some powerful diuretick, and if one might judge from appearances, the liquor had suffered no diminution in its double distillation; it is however, but fair to say, that the good dames of Telscombe conducted the process with as much modesty and decorum as their situation would admit of.

The Geneva drinkers exhibited 'modesty and decorum'
(SCM)

Tossicated

A Sussex man may be tight, or concerned in liquor, but drunk never!
(Thomas Turner)

To have a little beer means to have a great deal too much; to have half-a-pint otherwhile means to be an habitual drunkard; to be none the better for what he had took, means to be much the worse; to be nowadays tossicated implies abject helplessness.
(WD Parish)

Journalist Adam Trimingham in his book *Trimingham's Brighton* had this to say about a jolly civic knees-up:

> On the day he (George Lucraft) was made mayor in 1973 there was the usual banquet at the Royal Pavilion. As the throng stood for the loyal toast, a republican socialist called Arthur King (a highly appropriate name) refused to stand. The outraged and highly patriotic medical officer of health, William Parker, responded by pouring a glass of Yugoslav Riesling (that's what they drank at civic noshes in those days) over his head. Another socialist, Brian Finch, angrily poured *his* glass over the good doctor's head. It might have gone on in this way until the whole company was sloshed in more than one way had not everyone sat down again to join Councillor King and have a fag.

From the *Diary of Thomas Turner* of East Hoathly, August 30, 1758, after Turner had spent a night spent 'tippling' in Lewes with a Mr Gadsden:

> Weds. 30 Aug (1758). Came home in the norm about 6.20 ... Oh, how do I lament my misconduct! Sure I must be one of the worst

of fellows, so often as I have been overtaken in liquor, and that I still must remain so silly as I know even the smell of liquor almost makes me drunk that I should have no more resolution. What shall I do? I am even as it were drove to distraction ... Oh, the torments of a wounded conscience! ... I hope I may yet with the assistance of divine grace one day conquer my unruly passions, for without that I am sensible I can do no good thing. Dame Durrant dined with us on a hare roasted ... My wife a-picking of hops for Joseph Fuller in the afternoon, and I drank tea at Mrs. Weller's.

'He was so drunk he couldn't see through a ladder!' as they used to say in Sussex.

Writing of the days when 'Bright Young Things dashed down to the coast in their 3-litre Bentleys and boat-tailed Hispano Suizas', Raymond Flower, in *The Old Ship – a Prospect of Brighton,* told the story of the inebriate hotel guest who was shown up to his room, or what the porter thought was his room. Laid out on the bed was a dainty, lacy nightdress. 'The man took out his monocle and surveyed it solemnly. "What's this?" he asked."That," replied the porter, who was not sure whether the gentleman was expecting a lady or not, "is a lady's night-dress, Sir." The man leant over and put his nose to its scented folds. Then he turned to the porter. "Take it away," he commanded, "and fill it."'

Up until the 1960s one of the country reporters of the *Sussex Express* put in expenses for oats as he went about his district by horse, the reason being that he was most often falling down drunk and the horse knew the way home.

Robert Taylor, a Brighton Regency gent, had wined and dined well at Moulsecombe, a manor house a mile and a half up the road to Lewes. It was a moonlit summer night as he rode home and he was annoyed by a man who rode close beside him all the way. To escape, he galloped his horse to the Steine where, on stopping, he found he had been racing his own shadow.

A gentleman was driving along a country lane in the vicinity of Chichester's noted brewery, Henty's, when he saw a man, looking very ill, lying in the road on his stomach. He stopped his car and went over to the man.

'My poor man,' he said. 'Are you very ill; what's the matter?'

The man replied: 'There's nothing much the matter, sir, it's Colonel Henty got on my chest, an' I can't get 'im off yet.'

'Oh dear,' said the gentleman.

'And who be you, sir?' asked the victim.

'Well, I'm Colonel Henty!'

Lewes Lentils

In July 2001 Maude Cobb wrote to the letters page of the *Sussex Express*: 'Having recently moved to Lewes, I am looking forward to meeting someone who isn't an artist, or doing an aromatherapy course.' The following week, P Ulse responded with:

Lewes Lentilmobile
(New Age Eddie Card)

'It is only right to advise Maude, as well as other residents of Lewes, that some time ago an invasion of Earth took place by people from the planet Lentil. For some reason many of them settled in Lewes. I think you will find most of them, who I admit do have a passion for artwork and aromatherapy, are relatively harmless beings if left alone to go about their

business. Their dwellings can sometimes be recognised by the type of transportation outside, such as a 2CV car, a Land Rover with canvas roof, a cycle with a hatchling seat to the rear, or a tricycle with a shopping trolley attached. Most Lentils, as their name suggests, are non-carnivorous, but it is not uncommon to see them wearing leather sandals most days of the year. Sometimes you can spot them enjoying a light snack at the Grange Gardens, together with their hatchlings, after which they will dance merrily under the branches of the mulberry tree.'

Mr Ulse's description of certain Lewes residents (excluding natives of the town who, sensibly, moved to modern houses on the outskirts, enabling the Lentils to take over their crumbling little 'period town houses') is spot on. These tremendously worthy, caring people spend time out-reaching at alternative workshops, they campaign a lot both for and against things and like to become involved in arty projects involving the use of papier maché, foam and kitchen foil.

Millennia, the Long (expectant) Woman of Lewes – a companion, maybe, for the Long (emasculated) Man of Wilmington – was an interesting scheme proposed for the town. This hill figure of a naked, pregnant woman was intended for the steep grass slope on cliffs between The Snowdrop in South Street and Southerham

(Sussex Express)

Millennia

10

chalk pits. It was suggested as a work of art to attract tourism, celebrate the millennium and provide a focus for community activity (Lentil fertility ceremonies?). 'A pregnant figure would recall both the Madonna and pre-Christian Venuses,' it was claimed. 'The success of *The Kiss* exhibition shows how the association of a place and a sexual theme can be a strong attraction. The loss of *The Kiss* from Lewes (see below) reminds us to be bold.' Was the spokesman aware that the next valley to the north of the chosen greensward, just a few hundred yards away, is known to old Lewesians as

Fat Belly Woman

Fat Belly Woman (because of its rotundly suggestive topography)? Perhaps Millennia would have been more appropriately sited on the fat belly, or the thunderous thighs. Sadly, the Millennia proposal was not taken up.

Kate Fowler-Tutt, a Lewes headmistress and borough councillor, was a woman with strong views. It was she who objected to the realism of the original angels of victory on the town's memorial to the dead of World War One, and the angels' nipples were removed. Allegedly Miss Fowler-Tutt was also to blame for the loss to Lewes of a priceless work of art – Rodin's *The Kiss*, no less (or *one* of his stone osculations as, apparently, he made a number of copies). This statue shows the unclothed Paolo and Francesca from Dante's *Inferno*, and was commissioned by

11

aesthete Edward Perry Warren of Lewes House in 1904 for his partner James Marshall. The contract for Rodin stipulated that Paolo's genitals be depicted in precise detail. It may be that Warren and his friend lost interest and gave away the statue when they saw how Rodin had interpreted the order – the genitals are so rudimentary as to be practically non-existent. For whatever reason, the statue was offered as a gift to the town. Pleased with its cultural acquisition, the borough council made a special place for *The Kiss* in its elegant Assembly Room.

The year was 1915 and Lewes was awash with young soldiers. Girls hung around them like groupies and there were patrols outside the camps to turn them away. In *Sepoys in the Trenches* G Corrigan says that the impact of soldiery in general on Lewes was such that a bylaw was passed to prevent single women from being out on the streets after 8pm. Despite this, a letter to a Brighton newspaper in 1915 declared that 'Lewes is the most immoral town in England, and the Brighton area generally'.

Miss Fowler-Tutt tutted a great deal from the pulpit and the lectern about the morals of young girls. A clean-up campaign was launched. The council was embarrassed by the presence of the nude statuary in the Assembly Room, where dances and socials for the soldiers were held. How, though, could the town fathers (and Miss FT)

Inflamer of passions

12

point the moral finger with four and a half tons of sculptural 'pornography' on the premises? Under the guise of protecting it the council erected a fence and screen around the statue, but merrymakers still managed a peek. Eventually Warren was asked to take it back, which he did, parking it in his coach house. After his death *The Kiss* failed to sell at auction and finally found its way to The Tate. In 1999, now a priceless work of art, it returned briefly to Lewes for an exhibition, whereupon the then minister of the Jireh Chapel, keeping up a good Lewes tradition, said *The Kiss* was immoral as the stone duo were not married.

A Lewes citizen approached the local paper in 2001 to complain about the illegal dumping of a hefty 20ft 'cement mixer' on the foundations of a demolished prefab office building in the grounds of Lewes House (formerly Edward Warren's town house, and now headquarters of Lewes District Council). The paper asked the council what it was doing about such vandalism – only to be told it was a piece of council-approved sculptural art.

Sculptural art (Sussex Express)

In 1999 former Lewes man Matthew Dumbrell predicted the end of the world at precisely 1.50pm on August 5, two hours after that year's eclipse of the sun. He planned to return to his home town, having put his affairs in order, and await Armageddon on Mount Harry. When the world did not end he said he may have got his dates wrong.

Mooo

When, in 2001, Andy Treanor and Jo Harrington decided that their home – a terraced house plus former coach house in Elm Grove, Brighton – needed repainting, they considered the extended frontage too large for a solid block of colour and so went for a pattern.

And as the coach house had once been a dairy, a bovine theme seemed appropriate. Andy and Jo did the job themselves. Neighbours loved the friesian splodges, one saying it gave her boys street cred to live next door to the 'cow house'. Children returning from school like to congregate in front of the house and moo at it.

Can Can at the Duke's

High-kicking can-can dancer's legs, 20ft long, add a colourful note to the roof balcony of the Duke of York Cinema in Brighton.

They came to Sussex when Oxford picture house – Not The Moulin Rouge – closed in 1991.

(Photo courtesy of Mike Hemsley)

Daft old rustics

During the 1930s and 1940s the tremendously earnest *Sussex County Magazine* encouraged readers to submit humorous snippets. Almost without exception the stories were about daft old countryfolk, usually from the previous century. Few were funny and there was rarely a punchline (like the one about William Catt, owner of the tide mills between Newhaven and Seaford, who was said to be a stern man, 'so much so that one of his men is reputed to have said to him, "Gie us yer hand, sir – I love ye, I love ye, but I'm danged if I be'ant afraid of ye though".') Arthur Beckett, owner of the *SCM*, was enthusiastic about rustic Sussex humour, which he described as unconscious, distinct from wit and coming from a native shrewdness, 'a quality of the imagination that gives a fantastic turn to an idea' – or it could have been 'due to natural ignorance and lack of education and commonplace knowledge', he added. Few people outside Sussex found its rural humour in any way risible. It was said the anecdotes illustrated the stupidity rather than the wit of the rustics, and that any humour was 'extremely difficult to discover'. Whatever would those daft rural folk, whether shrewd or ignorant, and the equally silly toffs who perpetuated their utterances, have made of Swiss Tony and Edina Monsoon?

Oyez! Oyez! This is to give notice that Good Friday, coming on Friday, the market will be postponed to the day before.
(a Lewes Town Cryer)

Becket gave as an example the story of a Sussex man who, on seeing his doctor, was told he was suffering from erysipelas. Later he was asked by a friend what was the matter.

'I be sufferin' from 'Erry's shoes or 'Erry's slippers, but I baint sure which,' he replied.

The rector of St Nicholas in Brighton asked local fishermen why they did not come to church more often – St Nicholas being the only church in town then. They said: 'Well, sir, it be too far up the hill,' and the rector asked them if they wanted the church brought to them. Talking among themselves they thought this was a good idea and asked if they could slide the church down the hill on their boat slides. The rector jocularly said they could try, so a gang went up the hill with the levers and greasy slides they used for moving their boats up the beach.

Removing their coats and

Church of St Nicholas

Silly sayings

Everything in Sussex is a She, except a Tom Cat, and she's a he.

One boy is a boy, two boys is 'alf a boy, three boys is no boys at all!

Storrington people have to look in a puddle to see if it's raining.

Lewes folk are so mean they'd catch a rat for its hide an' fat.

Sussex folk are strong in the arm but weak in the head.

laying them in a row in the front of the church, they placed their slides in position and went behind to work with their levers. Some minutes later a man came along and, seeing all the coats in front of the church, made off with them. After perspiring at the back of the church one of the fishermen came round to the front to inspect progress and yelled: 'Whoa, we 'ave been and slid 'er on our coats; we'll 'ave to get 'er back!'

A new curate at Hurstpierpoint went to visit a dying parishioner whose bed had been taken downstairs to the parlour. He noticed a fine ham on the sideboard, upon which the invalid had his eyes. When the wife came into the room, the old man said: 'I would like a bit o' that 'am; I would like it so much!' His wife ignored the remark at first but when the poor old fellow asked again she turned to him and said: 'No, you can't have none o' that 'am; we're saving it up for your funeral!'

An old fellow with musical inclinations had taught himself to 'play' a violin. In his later years he became subject to severe attacks of asthma, and found that the cramped position of playing was having a serious effect on his disability. He looked at his fiddle and said: 'I'm growed out o' this 'ere thing, mother, I'll ha' t' git me a chello, I reckon.' 'What's the

18

good o' one o' them things to you,' she replied. 'You know you wouldn't ha' wind enough t' blow it.'

A farm-labourer used to tell stories of the wonderful cures made by a quack doctor in Cuckfield. He told how a sufferer went to the doctor on crutches, and 'the doctor took away the crutches, and told him to walk, and first he walked, and then he ran, and then he flew'. Asked what became of him, the man replied: 'Why, sir, someone with a gun could not make him out, and shot him!'

'All the folk I meet are unaccountable queer,' said a Sussex farmer to his wife. 'Yes, surelye,' she replied. 'All the world's queer except for us two, John, and there are times when I think that you're not quite so sane as you might be.'

A German fighter came down near a West Sussex village in 1941. 'The first person on the scene of the crash was, we heard, old Jarge, the shepherd, to whom various people at various times have unsuccessfully tried to explain that there is a war

Shrewd or silly?

19

on,' Anthony Armstrong wrote in *Village at War*. 'By unsuccessfully, I mean you can get the idea into his head one day, but he doesn't seem to realise that war isn't quite like rain or snow, something that may easily stop in the night. "What, be un *on* still?" he'll say when you next mention it.'

A walker arrived at a small hamlet and, seeking local information, asked the first person he saw: 'Are you a native of this place?'

'Am I a what?'

'Are you a native of this place?' the traveller repeated several times.

At which point the man's wife appeared at the door of her cottage and, after sizing up the situation, told her husband: 'Ain't you got no sense? He means was you livin' 'ere when you was born, or was you born before you began livin' 'ere.'

The passing of time was not measured by clocks and watches for old-time Sussex rustics. A labourer at Stantons Farm in East Chiltington was asked if he could remember the date of some event of recent happening. 'Yes,' he said, ''twere a fortnight ago come last Michaelmas twelve months.' Another man, asked to name the date when his last master had died, said: 'T'awd man died when our fourteen acres was wheat time afore last.'

A farmer's daughter met an old shepherd who had worked for her father for some years, and stopped to speak to him.

'I suppose you've 'eered tell 'bout my ole missus dyin', miss? 'Er passed away week ago las' Monday come nex' Froiday.'

A writer had occasion to revisit Brightling and an old wheelwright, whom he knew, was the first person he met on coming into the village.
'Hullo,' said the old-timer. 'I ain't sin yew sence last dungspreading.'

A pious woman remarked to her pastor: 'Praise be, I be still active for me years, for I be in my fower skore!'
'Four score!' exclaimed her pastor, 'you cannot possibly be so old!'
'Yes, I be, said the woman indignantly, 'I turned sixty to-day.'

Then there is the classic tale of the countryman who was proud of a 'rare timekeeper' of a clock. He said: 'When the hands of that clock stand at twelve, then it strikes two, and then I knows it's twenty minutes to seven.'

Marcus Woodward wrote of a labourer who knew neither his own nor his wife's age, nor could he remember her name. 'I calls her Paul,' he used to say.

In dialect

Benson's pig is Sussex dialect for the floor or ground; thus 'giving someone a close view of Benson's pig' means a thrashing.

You got up afore you went anywhere means you wasted time.

Nineways-for-Sunday means to look surprised; and nine times round a cabbage means a long time making a point.

21

A visitor enquired for Mr Pocock of Alciston of a local man, who replied: 'Never heered an him, an' doan know any sich pleace'.

After further enquiry it transpired that the local man was, in fact, Mr Pocock of Alciston.

When this was pointed out to him he said: 'You should ha' axed fur Mus Palk of Ahson.'

In his book *Forget and Smile*, about the Ditchling of his childhood in the early years of the twentieth century, Austin Shorney recalled the familiar sayings of farm workers.

Of poor children:

They ain't got a shoe to their feed nor a knicker to their behinds.

And of unmarried women:

Sh'em like a new, unfurnished cottage; never bin lived in.

A father of the bride asked the sexton at a country church about a peal of bells for the happy occasion. 'Do you want a tinkle or a blast?' the sexton said. Enquiring about the difference, the father was told: 'Well, if you want a tinkle, that's me, the missus an' de boy, an' dat'll be ten shillings, but if you want a blast, dat'll be all de lot an' us, and dat'll be thirty shillings!'

When an old farm worker had water laid on at his cottage his daughter asked him what he would do with his 100ft deep well. 'Cut it up and make holes of it,' he said.

Goin' up Lunnon

Writer EV Lucas, in *Highways and Byways in Sussex*, tells of the old lady who, in the early days of the nineteenth century, before she made her first visit to London, was asked what kind of place she expected to see. She replied: 'Well, I can't exactly tell, but I suppose something like the more bustling part of Ditchling.'

Marcus Woodward recounts the same story in wordier fashion, and adds: 'In Ditchling a dog might lie all day at the four cross-roads by the Bull Inn – the bustling part of Ditchling – and scarcely be disturbed by the traffic.'

When the staff of Allworks, grocers, of Battle, went for a day's outing to London some time in the 1930s, one of the younger workers found himself lost, so he asked a policeman in broad Sussex:

'Have you sin 'em den?'

'Seen whom?' the policeman said.

'Why Allworks men from Battle; they be up here somewhere.'

I justabout did enjoy myself up at the Cristial Palace on the Foresters' day, but there was a terr'ble gurt crowd; I should think there must have been two or three hundred people a-scrouging about.

An old Sussex farmhand was invited to London by his nephew. When he arrived at Victoria Station someone, seeing the old chap looking somewhat bemused, said cheekily: 'Hello! Come up to see the monkeys?'

'Yes, but I didn't think I should see one quite so quick,' the old man said.

Two visiting Londoners came across a Sussex man carrying a large pumpkin and asked him what it was. 'It's a mare's egg,' he said and happily agreed to part with it when the strangers asked if they could buy it. But the man carrying the mare's egg tripped and dropped it, and it rolled away down a hill until stopped by a bush. The rolling pumpkin frightened a hare which tore off, with the Londoners running in pursuit, yelling 'Stop our colt!'

In the 1930s there was an old keeper at Petworth, part of whose beat was an obscure wood, some miles from any road, called Goachers Furze. On his only visit to London the old man found himself in Parliament Square, facing the Palace of Westminster. He asked a Cockney what the building was, and the Cockney replied: 'You silly old fool, that is the Houses of Parliament.'

'Silly fool yourself,' said the old keeper. 'I bet if you came to Sussex you wouldn't know Goachers Furze.'

In court

Evidence given by a witness in a case of manslaughter: 'You see he pecked he with a peck, and he pecked he with a peck, and if he'd pecked he with his peck as hard as he pecked he with his peck, he would have killed he, and not he he.' (A *peck* is a pick axe.)

When a railway porter who had been employed at Arundel station pleaded guilty at the West Sussex Quarter Sessions (in 1947) to stealing mail-bags, it was stated that he was caught as a result of two detectives travelling in a mail van, hidden in labelled mail bags with slits cut for their eyes.

At the same sessions – when a prisoner was described by the medical officer of a mental hospital as a psychopath, the chairman asked: 'What is a psychopath?'

Counsel, playing for safety, replied: 'I think it is a medical expression, sir.'

By a flight of the imagination, the chairman was then able to define a psychopath as 'a workman who will work properly only if he has a foreman who knows his business'.

A doctor giving evidence in a drink-driving case, described the accused as 'truculent', and as breaking three matches while trying to light a cigarette. 'But he wrote rather more legibly than I do myself,' he very fairly added.

Prosecuting counsel: 'But you are, after all, a doctor.'

An old Pelham family retainer, ousted in his dotage from Halland Place on the border of Laughton and East Hoathly, was penniless and forced to claim parish relief. But from which parish? The two parishes resorted to the law to decide who would pay. It was discovered that when he was working at Halland Place, where most of his life was spent, the old man's bed was in East Hoathly, and it was judged that *that* parish would have to pay to look after the old man as his head had lain in East Hoathly when he was asleep.

Halland Place

The Jury do say that the sayd Thomas Palmer is guilty of the offence whereof he stands indicted in manner and forme contayned in the sayd indictment, thereof it is considered by the Court that he be thereof convicted and the sayd Thomas Palmer being present here in court and acknowledging he is not worth £20 is to be sett on the pillory in the market place in Lewes the next market day and to have both his ears nailed.
(Lewes Quarter Sessions, October 9, 1656)

Adam Trimingham tells this tale of Brighton coroner Ronald Webb.

Once he was conducting an inquest on a man who fell into a basement and died. The medical evidence revealed that he had suffered from every complaint known to man – cancer, heart trouble, diabetes, gout, arthritis, Parkinson's diesease, the lot. It was a wonder he was still alive before the fall, let alone afterwards. Webb took a full five minutes to write down this depressing catalogue of frailty. Then, whipping off his glasses with unexpected animation, he turned to the witness and said: 'Do you suppose, in your opinion, the deceased could have LEAPT to his death?'

At Horsham Assizes in 1664 Edward Baker was convicted of forgery and was sentenced to be:

... sett in and upon the pillory at Battle from eleven o'clock of the forenoon till one o'clock of the afternoon of the same day with a paper over his head showing his offence and have one of his ears cut off and also have and suffer one year's imprsonment without bail or mainprice.

An exemplary best man

(Puctures, Peter Cripps)

When self-proclaimed Goth, Peta Church, and Peter Stubberfield married in October 2003 they chose Elvis the ferret as best man for the Hallowe'en ceremony at Lewes Register Office .

Elvis and Lex

'We can't really have a wedding without a ferret,' said Peta, reasonably. 'So we're having two – Elvis and his son Lex.'

Peta found tiny tuxedos, bow ties and miniature hats for the furry duo and her only fear was that Elvis would eat his teeny-weeny buttonhole before the wedding began. In the event Elvis's behaviour was exemplary and he was the perfect best man, according to the happy couple, whose home is in Willingdon.

For the occasion Peta wore an elaborate, high-collared black dress set off with striking Gothic-style jewellery while Peter looked dashing in a scarlet Teddy Boy suit.

In print

Proof-reader Jenny Millington of Cooksbridge sent the following to the *Sussex Express* in December 1999, referring to a story the previous week about 'the dreadful effect of computer technology on typography', and bemoaning the loss of proof readers.

> *I have a spelling checker,*
> *It came with my PC,*
> *It plainly marques for my revue*
> *Mistakes I cannot sea.*
> *I've run this poem threw it*
> *I'm shore your pleased too no,*
> *It's letter perfect in it's weigh*
> *My chequer told me sew.*

Printer H P Clark was born in 'Brighthelmston, in the Hundred of Wales-bone in the County of Sussex' in September in 1797. After an indifferent education at various establishments around the town he joined his father in the turnery business. At thirty he left home to live in Rye where he set up his own turnery, and married. Two years later he decided to become a printer, even though he knew nothing of the trade 'because the only other printer in the town declined to print several things that were against the old currupt system carried on by the patron of the borough, Dr. Lamb'. Clark became known as a poet and writer, and in his book, cumbrously entitled *Clark's Guide to the History of Rye, to which is added its Political History, Interspersed with many pleasing and interesting incidents,* he gives an account of how he tried to cover his ignorance when he sought the advice of a type-founder in London about the equipment he would require.

'You will want,' he said, 'so much of Brevier, so much of Pica and so much of Fat-face Pica.' Here I was quite at a stand; Pica – I wondered what Pica meant. He still proceeded: 'So much of Great Primer, so much of Double Pica.' What! more Pica, thinks I. How I wondered what this Pica was; but I dared not show ignorance, having previously given him to understand that I had been in the trade. 'Well,' he proceeded, 'you will want so much Canon.' I nodded assent and was as wise as ever. 'So much of 4-line Pica, 6-line Pica, 8-line Pica, and 10-line Pica.' This was a stunner and no mistake. There were two things that I was sure of: that I knew nothing what Pica was, and that I shall never forget the name. 'Now,' says he, 'you will want some furniture.' But whatever furniture meant I knew not, it was equally as foreign as the rest – but there was no more Pica.

- *Pica is a size of type: furniture was the lead spacing used by compositors*

Head-bangers' trophy

A very special Jimi Hendrix air guitar, played by Ken Boulter alongside some of the world's greatest – including Eric and Keith – since Hendrix's death in 1970, is now on permanent display in the Six Bells at Chiddingly.

Ken, seen right in the picture, with landlord Paul Newman, decided his playing days were over and donated his precious instrument to the pub's popular music bar, which features both 'head-banging' air guitar gigs as well as live music.

The Hendrix guitar, which Paul is seen playing in the photograph, is in a glass display box in pride of place above the bar.

(*Sussex Express*)

31

Titillating titles

The Resistance of Piles to Penetration, *Elastoplast Techniques*, *Gay Gardens from Seed* and *Open-Air Pig Breeding* may never feature on airport bookstalls, but they and other agreeably silly-sounding books cause much merriment to passers-by in Lewes High Street. Michael Bell of Caburn Bookshop has a permanent window display of ludicrously-titled books, discovered in boxes of old volumes brought in for sale. Michael, the type of man whom Central Casting would produce for the part of the be-cardiganned, be-spectacled, *bookish* owner of a quaint old bookshop, exhibits a refreshingly ribald Sussex sense of humour. Here are some more of his fanciful tomes:

Caburn Bookshop

Single-Handed Cruising
Dick's Fairy
Muffs and Morals
The Captain's bunk, a Story for Boys
50 Faggots by Julian
The Art of Taking a Wife

How to Recognise Leprosy
  – a Popular Guide
When Men Wore Muffs
  – The Story of Men's Clothing
Pamela Pounce, a Tale of
  Tumultuous Petticoats
The Wise Virgin – The Missing Link
Between Men and Women
The Culture of the Abdomen; Cure for
  Obesity and Constipation
Creative Flash Techniques
Incurables and Humour
Turkey Plucking for Beginners
Advanced Camping in Lewes (1910)
Awful Disclosures of Marie Monk
The Romance of the Civil Service
Autobiography of the Best Abused Man in
  the World
The Pit Poets
A History of the Rod

Scientific Amusements
Hand Book of the Organ
British Tits
Scouts in Bondage
Chains and the Motorcyclist
Camp Songs
Menfrone: The One-Handed Monk
Young Man with a Horn
Totty, the Truth About Ten Mysterious
  Terms
Let's Toss For It
Leathers in Mozambique
Elementary Hyperbolics
Christie's Old Organ
Deviation and the Deviascope
My System for the Ladies
Swine Husbandry
Tossa

The piquant parson

Edward Boys Ellman (1815-1906), remembered still for his book *Recollections of a Sussex Parson* (1912) , was a grandson of John Ellman – the man who transformed Southdown sheep from thin, scraggy animals to the chunky, heavy-fleeced breed that became famous around the world. Edward was curate-in-charge, then rector of Berwick, a church with which he was associated for sixty-six years. A man ahead of his time, Edward had an almost contemporary sense of humour. Here is a selection of Ellmanisms.

The two Miss Shelleys of Lewes (relatives of Percy Bysshe) were among the town's notabilities. They prided themselves on their state of spinsterhood, and were very indignant at their sister for having married a Mr Dalbiac, it being 'an unheard of thing for a lady of the Shelley family to marry'. Wrote Ellman:

At the census of 1841, when the collector called for the paper, on looking at it to see whether it was filled up correctly, he noticed that the ages of the two surviving Miss Shelleys and of their three domestics were all stated to be twenty-five years. Whereupon the collector told the maid he should like to see her mistress. On being shown into her presence he said he thought there must be some little mistake as to the ages entered on the schedule, whereupon Miss Shelley indignantly said that she had never in her life met with such impudence as to ask the age of a lady! In that house they were all unmarried females, and that she could not think of putting each one down as more than twenty-five.

(A fortnight earlier, one of the Miss Shelleys had remarked to a visitor that they were very fortunate as they had not changed a servant for 'upwards of thirty years'.)

Contemporary with the Shelley sisters was Mrs Newton of Southover Grange – who was considered by all, not least herself, as the leader of Southover society (there being a Lewes society and a Southover society in the early years of the nineteenth century).

She always liked to go to the butcher's herself to choose her meat, and I have frequently seen her there with her basket of keys on her arm, which in the morning she always carried about with her. Later on in her old age she always had a chop at 2 o'clock, being waited upon by her old butler, who had been in her service upwards of thirty years. One day, just as time approached for the chop to be carried in, the old man suddenly dropped down dead. While the other servants were

Edward Boys Ellman
in old age

hastily considering how to break the information to their mistress, the bell was violently rung. On a servant appearing, the old lady demanded why the butler did not bring in her chop. On being told of his sudden death she merely said, 'That is no reason why I should be kept waiting. Is there not anyone else who can bring me my chop?'

Then there was the time Ellman went to tea with the wife of his churchwarden, William Stace, and Mrs Stace told him that if she ever came to poverty she would go to America and earn her living there by teaching languages to the natives. Her sister-in-law, Mrs George Stace, who was present, said she would like to go, too, and she would teach the poor natives how to make artificial flowers.

The Misses Tuttee, daughters of a clergyman, were staying at Glynde Bourne (Glyndebourne) during the time Ellman's grandfather, John Ellman, was living in the village. They complained to him about boys bathing within sight of the house, in a pond, and that it was a most indecent sight for any lady to see. 'The boys, on being spoken to, said they were so far off that they were sure the ladies could not have seen anything indecent, unless they stared at them through a glass.'

• A century later, Austin Shorney told a similar tale of a prim Ditchling woman complaining about naked boys and young men swimming in the Common pond. 'They're down there, masses of them, all in their bare pelts,' she said. Shorney wondered why she went that way so often.

The swine!

The Argus

UPPARK

SELSEY BILL

RYE

BEACHY HEAD

Sussex is pig-shaped, it's said, with the snout at Rye, the rear at Uppark and the legs at Selsey Bill and Beachy Head. And to match the county, the old Sussex breed were a pig-headed bunch who 'wunt be druv'. They would say: 'You may push and you may shuv, but I'm hemmed if I'll be druv.' 'Drackly' (directly) was the usual response of the pig-headed when asked to do something. It meant 'when I'm good and ready'.

The Reverend Coker-Egerton, one time Rector of Burwash, told of a freezing morning when one of his parishioners overtook a boy in a cart, sitting hunched up, thoroughly cold and miserable. 'If I were you, my little man, I'd get down and walk,' the boy was advised. The reply was, 'No, that I wunt. Not if I freezes fust.'

When around 1860 Tom Neeves, the village carpenter and painter at Brede, finished painting the Ten Commandments for Udimore Church, the vicar pointed out that he had done only eight. 'Ah well, I rackon there's as many up there as what you'll kip,' said pig-headed Tom.

Sussex stubbornness inspired W Victor Cook's poem *Sussex Won't Be Druv,* a composition that quickly achieved the status of county anthem.

Some folks as come to Sussex,
They rackons as they knows
A darn sight better what to do
Then silly folks like me and you
Could possibly suppose.
But them as comes to Sussex,
They mustn't push and shove,
For Sussex will be Sussex
And Sussex won't be druv.

(first of three verses)

On to other piggy aspects of the county. Anthony Armstrong tells the story of a neighbour who, during the Second World War, applied to the proper authorities for a young female pig so that there would be a plentiful supply of pork and bacon during hostilites. When the piglet arrived there were puppies in the household and the young porker grew up to think that she, too, was a dog. She frolicked with the pups and so often followed them when they went for their daily walk that the owner had to buy her a collar and a lead. The pig learned to come to the whistle and was soon as much a part of the family as the dogs. It was, of course, out of the question to eat her. The man from the pig authority arrived and asked to see the pig, expecting to be taken to a sty. The owner whistled and Frances Bacon galloped up. All the official could suggest was that the owner contact a pig farmer and breed from Frances. Unfortunately, Frances considered herself a dog and her romance with a neighbouring boar was short lived when she spurned him out of trotter.

(Bertrand Prance)

In his *Dictionary of the Sussex Dialect* (1875) the Reverend W D Parish recalled:

A parishioner of mine once came to complain to me that her husband had threatened to ill-use her on account of two little pigs which she was hobbing up; but as I found that his objection rested on the fact that she was hobbing-up the pigs so carefully that she insisted on taking them to bed with her, I declined to interfere.

• *Hobbing meant hand-rearing*

An old cottager in Green Street, Crowhurst, was awakened one bitterly cold night by someone knocking at his back door. The old man went downstairs and, on opening the door, was asked by the caller if he would help him to put a pig into a cart. Slipping on an overcoat, the cottager good-naturedly helped to load the pig, and even provided the lantern to throw light on the operation. When the pig was loaded the old man suggested a warming glass of his wife's home-made wine. The caller drank it and left with a cheery 'good-night', and the old man returned to his bed. Next morning he went to feed his sow, but found that the sty was empty.

Inn sign for the Runt-in-Tun pub in the Heathfield hamlet of Runtington.

A man who lived near the old forge in Brighton (it was among the fields then, at the top of the North Street area) had a pig that often escaped from its sty, so the old chap tied a knot in its tail to stop it getting through the hole.

Military manoeuvres

During the Second World War students of exclusive girls' school Roedean were evacuated to Keswick in the Lake District and, for the duration, the cliff top premises at Brighton became HMS *Vernon* (the shore-based training establishment had been bombed out of its original Portsmouth base). Two stories, possibly apocryphal, are told of the navy's occupation of the famous school.

In the sleeping quarters, above every student's bed was a bell and an ivorine label engraved with the legend 'Press the button if you need a mistress for any reason during the night'. It was said the young sailors needed no second invitation, but instead of 'the blonde brass of Betty Grable or the deep dark charm of Vivien Leigh' the restless sailor was more likely to be visited by an irate Chief Petty Officer who threatened unspeakable punishment 'if ever he pressed that ....ing button again'.

When the Navy arrived there were still a

Quarterdeck of HMS Vernon (Roedean)

few senior girls at Roedean, completing examinations. HMS *Vernon's* Commanding Officer, the story went, insisted that they leave before the sailors moved in. 'My girls will be all right; they've got it up here,' said the mistress in charge, tapping her forehead. 'Madam, it matters not where your girls have got it, rest assured my sailors will find it,' said the CO.

In the same war, Viscount Gage's stately ancient pile at Firle was occupied by the forces and, for a time, became Canadian Headquarters. Lord Gage was on active service with the Army and paid only fleeting visits to his home, but he remembered the Canadians well. He said:

> The First Canadian Division had more than the usual percentage of doubtful characters. The worst example of their behaviour was when they broke into the cellar and drank all my wine. I remember I had several dozen of excellent vintage White Burgundy, which they drank, so I was told, laced with gin. That was surely adding insult to injury.

Lord Gage recalled that the house became dirtier and more woe-begone, as time went on.

> Most of the balusters in the pine staircase disappeared, whether for burning or not was never established ... At one stage in the war a Canadian corporal was heard to remark: 'Firle is a dirty old dump. It must be fifty years old, and in Canada we would have pulled it down long ago.'

A Temporary Casualty

I knows a Sussex worthy
What b'aint the man 'e wor;
No more by day nor night can 'e
Tell of the the size 'e used ter be –
      (I'll say nor more'n that).
For why? They've put un out of sight;
An' all the yards 'e were in 'ight!

Of course 'e were a land-mark
Wid 'is two sticks an' all;
A reg'lar giant 'e were to see
There in the Downland chalk stood 'e
      (But say no more'n that)
For now to folkses satisfaction
They've fill'd un in, so's out of action!

But 'twon't be long I'll tell ye
Fore 'e's 'isself agen;

Sooner's was expected like
There'll be a resurrection like –
Come what may them Huns be done;
But not the Old Man of W--------n
      (Don't print no more'n that!)

Frank Hart, 1941

43

To the point

*Woman shopper
overheard in
Chichester during the
Second World War:
'If I could only have
my life over again, I
would spend my last
month's points
differently.'*

*An old lady from a
bombed Sussex village
was asked by a friend
if she was not terribly
frightened.
'Not so terribly,' she
answered. 'You see, my
grandfather was killed
at Waterloo.'*

During the 'doodle-bug season', according to Lord Winterton, the then member for Horsham and Worthing, one of the missiles fell near a Sussex farm cottage. All the windows were broken, the doors were jammed and most of the tiles came off the roof. The occupant got out through a broken window and hurried to the milking shed to see if his brother was all right. 'Well, I thought I 'eered some sort of a bang, and some of th' old cows was a bit tarrified,' said the cowman. 'But I went on with me milkin'.

An old man got on to a crowded bus in Chichester in 1944 and the conductor told a woman to take her small son on to her lap so that the pensioner could sit. The child 'howled and kicked and insisted he wanted a seat to himself'. The old man turned to him and said: 'You get all the oranges, and all the milk, and all the eggs, but you are not going to get this seat!'

In his village trilogy Anthony Armstrong wrote of the time he became officer in charge of the local Home Guard in a West Sussex village he called South Downing ('somewhere in Sussex', as they used to say in wartime; could it be South Harting?). He had collected together an assortment of farm workers, clerks, gardeners, domestic staff, shopkeepers, tradesmen and a 'gentleman of leisure', and came the red-letter day when he was called to draw rifles and uniforms.

Off I went and twelve long lumps of filthy grease were handed out to me, inside which were our rifles, the old P.14 type. In close and greasy proximity were twelve sets of denim overalls, blouse and trousers and forage caps ... That the good old Army was taking an interest in our existence and treating us as its own was soon apparent when we looked more closely at the uniforms. Nearly all the blouses were for six-foot men with forty-seven-inch chests, while the trousers were for fellows of at most five-foot-four with slim behinds like long-stemmed débutantes. They must have mistaken us for The First Loyal Neanderthals. However, we did a bit of swapping with another village, which couldn't get half its blouses on, though its trousers, even when braced tight under

First Loyal Neanderthals
(Bertrand Prance)

the armpits, still concealed its boots. They in turn had probably been mistaken for The First Loyal Sack-Racers. The Army's estimate of our average intelligence was also an unflattering one – all our first issue of caps being apparently for pinheads. Conversely the next lot fitted snugly down on to the shoulders.

One day Armstrong's troop, having learned how to make Molotov cocktails, went off to a secluded chalk pit to practice throwing them at a heap of old iron.

> 'This is a funny war. You can get stout, but you can't get fat.'
> Chalked notice on a house in Lickfold

The gallant Commander (myself) took it into his head at one point to dash nobly down and pick up someone's bottle which had only broken its neck and so wasn't burning properly, with the intention of smacking it down on the iron more effectively. He heaved it with such gusto, being also admittedly anxious to get rid of the darn thing as quickly as possible, that he did not notice that some of the contents whirled out behind him. *And on him!* Walking modestly back to his men he was quite unconscious that he was by then flaming away behind like one of Nero's Christian torches. He even took the shouts for applause. It was not till a fervent but indecorous cry from one of his less respectful Home Gardeners of, 'Sir, your arse is alight!' accompanied by a definite impression of extreme heat in an unusual place made him turn round – to find his backside well aflame and burning nicely. After smacking himself with more severity than he had experienced since the days of his last nurse some thirty-seven years previously, he finally had to plump down on the wet grass, where he held a regal sick-bed reception in a ring of laughing visitors, till he had gone out.'

A Hadlow Down yokel was sitting on a bench, pipe in mouth, on a beautiful spring day in 1940. He said to the old man next to him: 'What do you think of the war then, Bert?'

'It's lovely weather for it,' the other replied.

During the Second World War Ditchling was surrounded by encamped troops – British, American but mainly Canadian. There was a firing range on the Downs and, according to villager Leon Sinden, on one occasion a shell went astray and landed in the garden of Sir Stephen Demetriardi, who wrote a memo to the Commanding Officer saying: 'Sir, will you kindly explain a) why you are using my house as a target and b) why you are such a bloody bad shot.'

Rationing and shortages during wartime sometimes stretched a housekeeper's ingenuity to the limit.

A Chichester boarding-house owner bought a sheep's head from her butcher and asked him to leave the eyes in.

'It has got to see us through the week,' she explained.

Foibles of the famous

In *A Boy at the Hogarth Press* (1972), Richard Kennedy gives an account of his apprenticeship at Leonard and Virginia Woolf's printing and publishing house in London. The Woolfs invited sixteen-year-old Richard to their Rodmell home for a week-end, during which they took a stroll to Charleston Farmhouse to visit Virginia's sister, the painter Vanessa Bell.

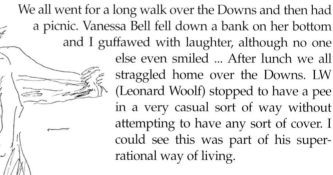

We all went for a long walk over the Downs and then had a picnic. Vanessa Bell fell down a bank on her bottom and I guffawed with laughter, although no one else even smiled ... After lunch we all straggled home over the Downs. LW (Leonard Woolf) stopped to have a pee in a very casual sort of way without attempting to have any sort of cover. I could see this was part of his super-rational way of living.

Mapp and Lucia author E F (Edward

(Richard Kennedy)

48

Frederic) Benson was Mayor of Rye from 1934 to 1937. A gentle humorist, Benson saw the funny side of most things. On being re-elected mayor for a second year he said, in his acceptance speech: 'I thank those present for the cordiality with which they approved of my return to this dignified but not very well upholstered chair.' Then, referring to a matter that had occupied the council during his first term – the planting of trees around the town – he added:

> No doubt you will remember a pamphlet written by Sir Samuel Hoare when he was Secretary of State for India. The subject of the pamphlet was re-afforestation, and he recommeded the planting of trees along the Ganges and other rivers. He said it would improve the climate and the view. Parliament turned it down, but after considerable debate the Town Council of Rye had decided to adopt this scheme for the afforestation of Romney Marsh. They haven't got very far with it yet, and I have not noticed that the climate has improved.

John Wyndham took his new bride to meet his Uncle Charles, Lord Egremont, at Petworth.

Turdiform

Ditchling author and artist Raymond Briggs castigated the former Kingswest Centre on Brighton seafront for its obscenely sausagey lettering, which he called 'turdiform'.

Poet Laureate John Betjeman accused the Ministry of Transport, in 1951, of erecting concrete lamp-posts across Sussex that 'looked like boa-constrictors being sick'

'Oh, what a beautiful lake!' she said. Thunder-laden silence. Then Uncle Charles spoke! 'My dear young lady, one day your husband will inherit from me not only all this, but also, among other things in Cumberland, half Derwentwater, the whole of Bassenthwaite Lake and the whole of Wast Water, comprising in all about thirty-five square miles of lake. What you see there is not a lake. It is a *pond*.'

The Dukes of Devonshire (the Cavendish family) acquired large areas of Eastbourne in the nineteenth century and developed it as a seemlier sister to bawdy Brighton. When the railway reached the town in 1849 the seventh Duke invested £37,000 in a sea wall and the sort of well-appointed houses that would lure the wealthy middle classes to the seaside. Within twenty years the resort grew into the 'Empress of Watering Places' and became the most resoundingly respectable and carefully laid-out new seaside town in Britain.

Through his agent, the Duke controlled the growth and character of Eastbourne to exclude the lower middle classes and the hoi polloi. Here, gentlefolk could 'decorously enjoy the high Victorian summers under the aegis of their ducal patron, who as the major local landlord, had ensured that their leases totally ruled out the display of washing in the gardens, the uncontrolled sale of alcohol or the faintest hint of industry or commerce in the residential quarters'.

Fancy that.

Cakes, Boers and flaming bums

Barcombe's Anthony Buckeridge, author of the Jennings books, was sent in 1920 to Seaford College when it was still in Seaford (later it moved to West Sussex). He was eight years old. He wrote of the primitive conditions (three buckets beneath holed-out seats, bread and scrape for tea).

We had our birthday cakes sent from home; these wonderful confections of icing and marzipan were the ultimate reward or threat to anyone hoping for a slice. There was, however, a terrible disaster one day when a boy took his birthday cake up to the master on duty to ask for permission to take the cake, already sliced, to his friends at other tables. It so happened that the headmaster made one of his rare appearances in the dining-hall and was chatting to the matron and master on duty at the top table. The boy (it could have been Woodhams or Doyle or possibly Walters) stood behind the master awaiting an opportunity to make his request. The headmaster turned and saw the boy waiting patiently at his elbow. 'Ah, Woodhams! (or Doyle or possibly Walters) Is that for me? How kind of you.' He then took a slice and treated himself to a bite. 'A beautiful cake! Don't you agree, Matron?'

Matron couldn't say, not having tried it, so she had to be offered a slice – so, too did the master on duty. Walters (or Woodhams *et al*) stood paralysed with horror as three precious slices disappeared down the throats of adults who should have known better. After the meal, Woodhams (or whoever) was confronted by three furious cake-less claimants thwarted of their expectations by this outrageous act of sabotage.

This was told by a Ditchling man who was six at the time of the Siege of Ladysmith, 1899.

We was all in the class, and sir said that some farmers called Boers had some of our people held captive-like, in siege, so we must all pray for their safe release. After school finished we talked it over like, one boy he sayed 'Mase Mugridge he wouldn't do a thing like that.' 'No,' said another, 'but what about Abergavenny then?' 'Nah,' said one, 'he bain't a Boer he be a Marquis.' Then I sayed, 'It be them buggers up at Westmeston'. So we all agreed, no use praying, we'd go up and release them ourselves. So armed with sticks we raced across the fields and we saw nary a soul. The others looked at me, an' I thought quick like, and said they've taken them up the lime kilns, we've no hope of getting them out of there. So we let out all the pigs and chickens just to give them Boers something to think about, then we scarpered back. It was some years before I learnt the Boers weren't even English.

More Buckeridge:

Confirmation classes were taken by the local curate (J Taylor Whittle), but on the day before we were confirmed there was an unvarying ritual. One by one the cadidates were summoned to the HM's study for a man-to-man initiation into the world of human sexuality, of which it was tacitly assumed that we knew nothing. The proceedings went like this:

'Well, Buckeridge, you are growing up now. I don't suppose you know how you were born, do you?'

'No, sir.' This was the obligatory reply.

'It's like this. When a mother and father decide to start a family, the man passes the seed to the woman, and in the course of time a child is born. Any questions?'

'No, sir.'

'Right! Send the next boy in.'

I went out trying to visualise a highly-coloured packet of sunflower seeds being handed from husband to wife across the dining-room table.

Writing about old time rustics' apparel in *SCM* in 1934, R J Sharp said:

Parlez vous?

In April 2002, teachers at Lewes Old Grammar School produced a list of useful phrases for pupils about to make a trip to Dieppe. One was 'Je peux trouver mon chemin au port sans ces menottes pour vous remercier', which translates as 'I can find my way to the port without these handcuffs, thank you.'

The modern corduroys are not so strong smelling as the old, which I heard accounted for by the fact that formerly dogs' urine was used in the process of manufacture, it being collected in 'iron bottles' and sold to the northern manufacturers. I remember when Christ's Hospital (a boys' school) was being removed from London to Horsham, the boys were boarded out at other schools for a term. We had one at our school and he, before taking into wear a new pair of his velveteen breeches, hung them out of the window several nights to get the smell out of them, which he said was the usual procedure, and if the frost could be got on them, so much the better.

Merry Rushton, a Roedean pupil from 1948 to 1954, threw light on the innocence of (some) teenage girls in the middle years of the last century with this contribution to *Memories of Roedean*:

After a summer half term at home I said to our gang of seven: 'Girls ... I hardly know how to tell you this – but Mummy and Daddy do it for fun!' ... The stunned expression on all their faces, and the silence which followed, is remembered by every single one of us to this day. After a few seconds one recovered enough to say, 'Well, mine certainly don't', quickly followed by the others – 'Nor do mine!', 'Or mine!' Then a kind girl said: 'Look, girls, I don't think this ought to make any difference to our friendship with Merry.' After a moment's hesitation they all, one by one, generously agreed. Many times after that my parents sat in the gallery of the Chapel happily ignorant of the fact that at least seven pairs of adolescent eyes were boring in to them. My mother had said something like 'it's a very happy thing to do', but we all thought you only 'did it' once to have a baby.

At a scout troop camp at Glyndebourne between the world wars Owl patrol enjoyed a fiery entertainment. Austin Shorney wrote, in his memories of childhood:

One boy, who had developed the ability to contain considerable amounts of wind, apparently saved up for some hours, and when all was ready, a lighted match was applied and the expelled methane lighted up like a flare. The boy whose prowess was thus displayed could never be persuaded to give a repeat performance, because the flame had backtracked fast to the source of its fuel and the sudden unexpected singeing he had received did not encourage him to do it again.

Shorney's friend Pat Cundy lived with his family in a wooden bungalow at Wivelsfield. They were railway mad and had shelves round the walls with holes cut between rooms so that an extensive model railway layout could be operated. 'You might be looking at a book in Patrick's room when suddenly the Royal Scot would thunder in at one side, speed along a wall, and leave through a gap near the door. They even had a railway signal outside the lavatory which you pulled up when you went in and let down when you had finished, if indeed you could finish with a couple of fast LMS goods trains shooting past the back of your head.'

Archaeological find of the century

In the spring of 1983 a sensational archaeological discovery in Lewes was revealed when *News in Focus*, the *Kent and Sussex Courier's* free newspaper, announced that the remains of William de Warrene – the Norman who built Lewes Castle in the eleventh century – had been found buried, and seated on a horse, beneath Brack Mount. The mount is the castle's second motte.

After a landslip on the mount, John Owen, landlord of the Lewes Arms, discovered the keystone opening to a collapsed chamber while clearing fallen rubble in his yard. The Sussex Archaeological Society was alerted, a secret excavation began and artefacts found in the chamber confirmed it was indeed the earl's grave.

The discovery was said to confirm the authenticity of William's will in which he left detailed instructions for his heart to be buried in the Priory of St Pancras alongside the tomb of his wife, Gundrada, and for his body, in full armour, seated on his favourite charger Norman, to be buried at some other unspecified place. Until then historians had always regarded the will as a fake – and they believed that the earl's tomb was destroyed when the Brighton-Lewes railway was laid through the Priory ruins in the 1840s.

Heralding the discovery as the archaeological find of the century, historian Dr Graham Mayhew said it would rank with the discovery of Eoanthropus Dawsoni. He added: 'The mount is clearly Lewes's tribute to Earl William. The townspeople must have raised this massive burial mound in gratitude to a conqueror turned civic benefactor. It has always been assumed that Brack Mount was an early motte of Lewes Castle. Now we know the truth.'

In charge of the excavation was Mlle Avril Betise, an eminent archaeologist from Rouen, whose special study was the Normans in Sussex; her discoveries included a significant haul of artefacts.

'I understand the value of some of the objects is substantial,' Mr Owen said. 'I hope eventually to have a set of replicas made for the front bar which I am considering renaming the Earl William bar.'

The first person to suspect something dodgy about the April 1 story was nurse Thea Petch, who was on the phone a matter of minutes after her paper was delivered.

A week later *Focus* confessed all and, ironically, co-conspirator John Owen then had an anxious moment when a rival prankster belaboured him publically for 'excavating' Brack Mount – a scheduled ancient monument.

Mlle Avril Betise with Dr Mayhew (centre) and Mr Owen on the site of what the historian called 'the find of the century'

... but mostly cricket

Edward Boys Ellman (again) had a fund of funny cricket stories, some of which are:

I remember one occasion when my father, hearing that there was to be a (cricket) match at Seaford between Public and Private School men, drove over to witness it. On appearing on the ground he was at once seized upon by the Public School team (he had been at Winchester) and entreated to play, as one of their number had at the last moment suddenly failed them. He pleaded that he had given over playing for many years. Then he pointed out a piece of water, which he said did not allow of a large enough field. Both sides laughed at the idea of the possibility of sending a ball as far as the water. In the end my father was persuaded to play. When batting, on the first opportunity he had, he sent his ball into the middle of the sheet of water, where it could be seen floating about, and so could not be called a lost ball. On that ball my father obtained twenty-four runs before anybody waded into the water after it.

Henry Hurley, one of the partners in the Lewes Old Bank, was playing cricket on the summit of Cliffe Hill one day when he sent the ball so far that it rolled down the steep hill. A fielder went after it, and another stood by to catch it – but not having a firm footing, he missed, and the ball went back to the bottom. Up it went again, and once more the catcher missed it. At last the fielder climbed up the hill with the ball in his pocket, by which time an exhausted Hurley had made more than seventy runs.

There was a man ... who offered to meet and beat any four players belonging to the same family. His family team consisted of himself, his wife, his boy and his dog. His dog was a splendid fielder and quite entered into the game.

Glynde archivist Andrew Lusted interviewed old-timer George Miller in 1988, and so happened upon the game of Fat, as played in the Trevor Arms every Sunday morning. How does it go, Andrew enquired.

Out for a duck – scoreboard spotted in the 1950s on the Poynings to Edburton road

Fat? Well, it's nines and fives . . . You've got the ten wallah and the eighteen wallah, which is the five and the nine of the suit you've made trumps. If you made clubs trumps, the five of clubs was ten and the nine of clubs was eighteen. That's how you peg it, on the peg-board you see. And you peg eighty-eight. After you've finished your hand you count up. Ten is ten and you make eighty-eight of it all the time, see. It's an interesting game, like. I used to like a game of Fat. Nobody can play it now.

Alley, tolley and bosser

The World Marbles Championship takes place in Sussex, at Tinsley Green. Here, the Gentlemen of the George play at Battle on Good Friday.

Lord Egremont and his heir, John Wyndham, were hunting near Petworth in 1940. They were casting about for a lost fox when they heard 'a tremendous hullabaloo about two miles away'. They galloped in the direction of the noise and came upon a village football match. Wrote Wyndham:

The hounds, the huntsman, the whipper-in, Uncle Charles and I all slithered to a stop. The footballers and the bystanders who had been making the noise all stopped too. There was silence, then Uncle Charles, who had turned red in the face, stood up in his stirrups and shouted: 'Haven't you people got anything better to do in wartime than play *football*?' We then went on hunting.

'Plant was rooted to the spot' – from a *Littlehampton Gazette* football report.

Although beaten hollow at every game we English have ever invented we can still show the rest of the world a clean pair of heels at one or two of the more obscure sports. Take the Tommy Trott Beer Race at the Laughing Fish pub in Isfield on Easter Monday. Dozens of people trot through the village, each carrying half a pint of ale. The winner is the trotter who loses the least beer. The race was started in 1956 by landlord, Tony Trott. This picture comes from the 2003 race, which was won by Ian Moore.

Sussex Express

ca scoops pea title

Not quite champagne: Winner Alex Siewert (centre) celebrates with Da...

'America scoops pea title' says the headline on this *Sussex Express* report of October 2002. Alex Siewart from California, obviously infected with Sussex silliness, became the first non-Lewes winner of the World Pea Throwing Championships at the Lewes Arms. He took the world record with a throw of 34.57 metres.

Weep-Not, it could be worse

Some of Sussex's Puritan composite baptismal names of the seventeenth century (and a few from the century before) reveal a strange eccentricity. These were people who changed their names from the perfectly respectable John, Henry, Edward, William, Sarah, Anne and Hannah and so on, which they regarded as heathenish, to others 'more sanctified and godly'. How daft is that?

Fly Fornication Richardson of Waldron was perhaps the most ludicrous. Then there were Performe-thye-vowes Seers of Maresfield, a Roundhead captain called Kneel-to-God Blades, More-Fruits Fowler of East Hoathly, Redeemed Compton of Battel, Stand-fast-on-high Stringer of Crowhurst, Weep-Not Billing of Lewes, Called Lower of Warbleton, Elected Mitchell of Heathfield, Renewed Wisberry of Hailsham, The-Peace-of-God Knight of Burwash, Fly Debate Joiner of Brightling and Kill-sin Pimple of Withyham. How were they addressed by friends and family? 'Hi, Weep-Not.' 'Yo, Renewed.'

Just as potty were Be Thankful Maynard of Brightling, Be Courteous Cole of Pevensey, Safety-on-High Snatt of Uckfield, Search-the-Scriptures Moreton of Salehurst, Ffreegift Mabbe of Chiddingly, Increase Weeks of Cuckfield, Seek Wisdom Wood of Waldron, Fight the Good Fight of Faith White of Ewhurst and Small Hope Biggs of Rye. Arlington had Sin-Deny Earle, Zealous Foote and No-merit Vinall. At Northiam, the rector John Frewen baptised his sons Accepted and Thankful. Accepted Frewen became Archbishop of York in 1660.

The Sussex bit of the road

'Why is it that the oxen, the swine, the women, and all other animals, are so long-legged in Sussex? May it be from the difficulty of pulling the feet out of so much mud by the strength of the ankle that the muscles get stretched, as it were, and the bones lengthened?' This from Dr John Burton in his 1751 book *Iter Sussexiense* (a tome written in Latin and Greek and translated for silly Sussex by W H Blaauw). Burton came to Sussex to visit his mother, who had married the rector of Shermanbury, and found:

> . . . a muddy, fertile, and pastoral country, smooth and flat indeed, when seen from afar, but not easy to ride or drive through; so that, having thereby earned a bad name, it has passed into a by-word, and any difficulty hard to get through, or struggle against, may, by a simile, be called the Sussex bit of the road.

There is an apocryphal (one hopes) story of a traveller who came across a hat lying in the mud. When he lifted the hat he found a man beneath it. Asked if he required assistance, the buried man said: 'Never mind me, look to my horse.' When excavated the horse was found to be feeding from a cartload of hay lost the previous day.

Cheesy feet

To stop their feet from getting dirty on the way to church, the Jefferays of Chiddingly had a line of cheeses laid as stepping stones from their mansion to the church door. The Jefferay monument in church shows two of the marble figures standing on round tablets like huge cheeses.

Lord Chancellor Cowper, in a letter to his wife in 1690, wrote:

I write to you from this place as soon as I arrive, to tell you I have come off without hurt, both in my going and return through the Sussex ways, which are bad and ruinous beyond imagination. I vow 'tis melancholy consideration that mankind will inhabit such a heap of dirt for a poor livelihood.

In 1829 Edward Lear visited Peppering House near Barpham, where the awful roads inspired his poem *Peppering Roads*.

> *If you wish to see roads in perfection,*
> *A climax to cart ruts and stones;*
> *Or if you have the least predilection*
> *For breaking your neck or your bones;*
> *If descents and ascents are inviting,*
> *If your ankles are strangers to sprains,*
> *If you'd cure a penchant for sliding,*
> *Then to Peppering go by all .*

Rollicking reverends

A friend and neighbour of that fine raconteur, Edward Boys Ellman, was William Douglas Parish, vicar of Selmeston and Alciston, another clergyman with a well-developed sense of the

William Parish

ridiculous. Parish was what Ellman called 'a confirmed bachelor', most certainly in the old-fashioned sense of the phrase. He wrote:

Once I tried hard to persuade Parish to subscribe to the Clergy Widows' Fund for the Lewes Archdeaconry, of which I have so long been secretary. He refused on the grounds that he was helping the society already by not marrying.

On one occasion, to his delight, a bill was sent in to him in all good faith by a London firm, for a large amount for doing up Mrs. Parish's sealskin jacket. Instead of writing back and saying there was no Mrs. Parish, he wrote to the firm to say it was a mistake, as Mrs. Parish did not possess a sealskin jacket.

Parish, appointed Chancellor of Chichester Cathedral, was at work in the cathedral library one day, and was disturbed by cacophonous noise from the organ, which he imagined was being tuned. He called one of the vergers and asked him to tell the organist to put off the tuning until he had finished his work. The verger informed him that an organ recital was going on.

Bishop Gilbert of Chichester loved to tell of the time that Mrs Gilbert went to the Royal Academy, just before opening day, 'being desirous to obtain a private view'. But she was refused admittance by a policeman at the entrance. She told him she was the Bishop of Chichester's lady. 'Even if you had been the Bishop's wife you could not go in,' was the answer.

A later Bishop of Chichester, Bishop Durnford, was at a dinner where another bishop told how, after one of his sermons, the alms bags were choked with offerings 'and ladies took off their jewels to give to the collection'. In the silence that followed, Bishop Durnford asked in a stage whisper: 'Could you lend me that sermon?'

Jevington church prided itself upon being very musical. Some time in the 1830s parishioners decided to have an organ, of the wind-up type. Since a wagon had to go to London to fetch the organ, a local farmer's wife arranged to have a washing machine sent from the city at the same time. Saturday night came, and with it the wagon. It was late, and by mistake the washing machine was put in the church, and the organ left at the farm – as you'd expect, this being that kind of story. But early next morning the mistake was discovered, and an exchange made in good time for the service. A large congregation assembled. When a psalm was given out, the organ was wound up and performed beautifully to accompany the hearty singing. After four verses the congregation stopped singing, but the organ went on. In a fluster the man in charge forgot what he had to turn or push, but he did something, and the psalm tune changed into *Drops of Brandy*, a popular and vulgar song of the day. He had another go and the tune changed into *Go to the Devil and Shake Yourself*. Frantic efforts were made to stop it before the organ was carried out to the churchyard where it played itself out. Another version of this same story had the rector running down the lane with the organ still playing and then throwing it into the village well.

- *These organs usually had three psalm tunes and a wider selection of secular tunes.*

One hot summer's evening a seaman from one of the ships at Portsmouth sauntered into the church at Bosham. The singing of the hymn before the sermon evidently attracted him. The Rector was in one of his theatrical moods, for he had no sooner ascended the pulpit than he thundered forth without quoting chapter or verse: 'Who will go with me to Ramoth Gilead?' A short pause, then again, in a still louder voice: 'Who will go with me to Ramoth Gilead?' The seaman, a simple fellow, responded to the appeal. He stood up and called out: Take me y'r Reverence, if it ain't too far. (August Hare in *Sussex*, 1894)

The Reverend H F Tomkinson, vicar of St John's Church in Hove (where his colleague was Canon A J Toop), bemused by correspondence addressed to them, noted, in 1948:

> We are indeed well staffed. Besides Canon Toop and myself, the following clergy also officiate at St John's. Canons Troop, Toupe, and Tupe; and Messrs Tompkinson, Tompkins, Thompkins, Thompkinson and Tompison. And sometimes, by special epistolary courtesy, the envelope is for one of them, and the letter for another.

In the days before the turnpike via Ranscombe Hill linked Lewes to Beddingham, the route went round by Glynde. A Lewes preacher was engaged to take the service at Beddingham one Sunday. There used to be a plank across the river for foot passengers, but no regular track. This was the route taken by the clergyman. He crossed the plank all right, but on attempting to jump a brook fell in. Meanwhile the congregation was waiting in the church. The clerk went looking for the missing reverend and returned to announce: 'There will be no service to-day, for the parson has fallen into a dick.'

A similar story, possibly of the same occurrence, has the clergyman falling from his horse into a water-filled ditch. Saturated, he said he was unable to preach. The clerk announced to the congregation: 'Ye-be to goo now, Passon ant a-gooin' to preach to-dey acause he's wet 'is-self'.

This story comes from John Wyndham's *Wyndham and Children First*:

It fell to Uncle Charles, as patron of the living of Petworth, to appoint a rector there. The clergyman arrived with a groom-gardener and a house-parlourmaid. This was at the beginning of the present century (twentieth), and the rector's staff was for those days considered very modest. Soon after the rector had installed himself, he saw a party of woodmen preparing to cut down a yew tree in the churchyard. 'Who sent you to cut down this tree?' he enquired. Uncle Charles, they said. The rector, declaring that the business of the churchyard was his business and nobody else's, sent them away. So off they went to the Estate Office and reported what had happened to the head forester, who told it to the chief clerk, who told it to the agent, who told it to his Lordship, who wrote a note to the rector and gave it to the butler, who gave it to the first footman, who gave it to a boy who took it to the rector.

Uncle Charles's note said: 'Dear Rector, I shall be obliged if you would not interfere with my servants when they are carrying out my instructions.'

The rector wrote back: 'Thank you for your letter. I shall send round my groom-gardener and my house-parlourmaid to cut

Rev counter

In the early nineteenth century few of the clergy who ministered in the villages around Lewes area actually lived in their parishes. In fact, so many of them rode out of town in their black coats on Sunday mornings that Lewes was nicknamed The Rookery. By association Lewes people became known as the Rooks –and subsequently the town's football club players were dubbed the Rooks.

So kind ...

The minister of a Sussex church, on leaving after some years of faithful service, was presented with two pounds of apples from the Harvest Thanksgiving, for which he sent the following letter: 'Dear Friends, I am preserving the rind of the admirable fruit you have given me, as it is the only token of remembrance that I possess, and one so suitable of a generous and grateful church.'

down the big cedar tree on your south lawn. I shall be grateful if you will not interfere with my servants when they are carrying out my instructions.'

The Reverend Richard King-Sampson, Curate of Hooe, told of two sisters who were to be married by his predecessor in the 1830s. The vicar knew them, but did not know the bridegrooms. When the service began the bridal pairs were wrongly sorted, but not knowing this the old vicar proceeded to marry them. Each couple repeated the vows, but the men changed names. Afterwards, in the vestry, the mistake was discovered. 'Please sir, you have married us to the wrong girls,' said one of the bridegrooms. The vicar was at a loss as the marriage was completed, except for the signing of the register. The bridal party asked for a little time to talk the matter over while the vicar paced up and down outside. When he was called back to the vestry the quartet said they had talked the matter over and that the marriages would do very well as they were, for they had all known one another so long that it did not matter who married whom.

A newly-married couple bought a house in the Sussex countryside. After inspecting it they realised they hadn't seen a WC, so they wrote to the local vicar, who had shown them over the property, asking if he knew where it was. The vicar, thinking they meant Wesleyan Chapel, replied: 'The WC is seven miles from the house. This is unfortunate if you are in the habit of going regularly. However you will be pleased to know that people take their lunch and make a day of it. By the way, it is made to seat 300 people and the committee has decided to fit plush seats to ensure greater comfort.'

A Sussex sporting parson once wished to attend some Monday races at Worthing, and in order to be in time he knew he would have to leave for Worthing on the Sunday afternoon, which meant that he could not take the usual service. He told his clerk to announce in church on Sunday morning that the second service would not be held, but not to give the reason. But the clerk misunderstood, for when the time arrived for the giving out of church notices, the parson was horrified to hear the clerk say: 'This is to give notice that there won't be no sarvise this afternoon, 'cos parson be agwine to Worthing to be in time for races to-morrow marnen.'

'If the individual who appears to find difficulty in reversing his vehicle without backing through The Vicarage fence will call at The Vicarage, the Vicar will gladly give him driving lessons.'

Offer from the Reverend D J Macgregor, Vicar of Chiddingly, in a 1943 parish newsletter

The Reverend Owen Vidal, who was the first incumbent of Dicker church in 1840, and his twin brother, James Henry, who was also in holy orders, had never been separated, either at school or at college, and they were so much alike that they were often mistaken for each other. At a Chapter meeting at Firle a Mrs Hutchinson asked Owen Vidal: 'Is it you or your brother?' Owen answered: 'It's my brother, ma'am.'

Also on the subject of God's house – Sunday School teacher Jacalyn Boyes went along to St Mary's in Kemp Town, Brighton, armed with enthusiasm and a rocket. The theme that Sunday was the Ascension and Jacalyn intended letting off the rocket with a picture of Jesus taped to it to illustrate His Ascension into Heaven. The rocket was duly sent up outside St Mary's and the children were filled with excitement as it exploded in a multitude of stars. No sooner had they gone back inside when in walked two uniformed police officers. There had been complaints. Fearing arrest, Jacalyn explained about the Ascension. Said one of the policemen: 'Well, if you sent the rocket up to Jesus, then I'm sure He will find it in His heart to forgive you.'

Inscription on a brass in Selmeston church, dated 1639:
...the body of Henry Rogers, A painfull preacher in this church two and thirty yeeres.

In the twelfth century any whale washed up on a part of the shore belonging to the diocese of Chichester belonged to the diocese, Pope Eugenius III decreed. Except the tongue, which belonged to the king. But if a whale were washed up on any other part of the Sussex shore, all the diocese was entitled to was the right flipper.

Signs of the times

Cooley, a Lewes barber, was famous for his anecdotes. He had a shop in the High Street, decorated with a sign showing Absalom hanging by his long hair to the bough of a tree while his horse galloped away. Accompanying the illustration were these words:

> Oh, Absalom, unlucky prig!
> Hadst thou but worn a periwig,
> For had thy luckless head been shaved
> Thy life most surely had been saved.

The following, said to be the words on a village sign of 1786, appeared in *Sussex County Magazine* in 1935 as 'an example of Sussex humour', although the contributor, while guaranteeing it to be a fact, failed to say which village.

> Isaac fac totum, barber, Perri-wig maker, Surgeon, Parish Cleark, School mester and blacksmith and man-midwife, shaves for Penny, Cutts hair for Towpence and oild and Powders into Bargain, young Ladys genteley edicated, Lamps lited by the head and quarter, young gentlemen also taut Their grammar language in the neetest manner and

great care taken of their morrals and spelin also salme singing and horse shewine by the real maker, Likewise makes and mends all sorts of butes and shoes, teaches the hoboy and Jews harp, cutts corns, bledes and blisters on the lowest terms, blisters and purges at a penny a piece, con-tillion and other dances taut at home and abroad, Also deals holesale and retaile perfumary in all its branches, Sells all sort stationry wair with blacking balls, red herrings, ginger bred and Coles, scribbin brushes, treycle, mouse traps and other sweetmetes, Likewise Potatoes, sassages and other garden stuff.

Here is another, allegedly seen in a curiosity shop in East Grinstead's High Street.

ROGER GILES, Surgin, Parish Clark and Skulemaster, Groser and Hundertaker, Repectably informs ladys and gentlemen that he drors teef without wateeing a minit, applies laches every hour, blisters on the lowest tarms, and visicks for penny a peace. He sells Godfathers kordales, kuts korns, bunyons, dotersh hosses, clips donkies wance a month, and hundertakes to luke arter everbodies nayls by the ear. Joesharps, penny wissels, brass kannelsticks, frying pans and other moozical hinstrumints hat grately redooced figers.
   Young ladys and gentlemen larnes their grammar and a langeeuadge in the purtiest manner, also grate care taken off their morrels and spellin. Also zarmzinging, tayching the base vial and all other zorts of fancy work, squadrills, pokers, weazels and all country dances tort at home and abroad at perfeckshun. Perfumery and snuff in all its branches.

As times is cruel bad I beg to tell ee that i has just beginned to sell all sorts of stashunary ware, cox, hens, vouls, pigs and all other kinds of poultry. Blackin briches, herrins, coles, scrubbin brishes, traykel and godley bukes and bibles, mise traps, brickdust, whisker-seeds, moreel pokkerancherchers, and all zorts of swatemaits, including taters, sassagers and other garden stuff, bakky, zizars, lamp oyle, tay kittles and other intozzikatin likkers, a dale of fruit, hats, zongs, hare oyle, pattins, bukkits, grindin stones and other aitables, korn and bunyon zalve and all hardware.

I has layed in a large azzortment of trype, dogs mate, lollipops, ginger beer, matches, and other pikkles, such as Hepsom salts, hoysters, Winzer soape, anzetrar.

Old rugs bort and sole here and nowhere else, new layde heggs by me, ROGER GILES: zinging burdes keeped sick as howles, donkies, paykox, lobsters, crickets, also a stock of selebrated brayder been bort up.

P.S. – I tayches gography, rithmetic, cowsticks, jimnastics and other chynese tricks.

An advertorial – an advertisement in a newspaper, presented as proper news – is not a modern wheeze, for it was much in use in the eighteenth century. Here's one from the *Sussex Weekly Advertiser* of June 24, 1782:

Last Monday one Turner, at Buxted, in this county, drank, as a specific for an Ague, nearly a quart of geneva, with an ounce of pepper infused therein, which operated so

Mating toads on the roads

Warning for drivers passing through Litlington that hoards of amorous toads were migrating across the road during the mating season to reach their spawning ground.

powerfully upon him that he was found dead the next morning in his bed. To prevent the ignorant from falling victims to such-like mortal potions in future, and to warn the public against the imposition and danger of ignorant Empirics in the above disorder, Dr. Thompson's Tincture is recommended, which experience has proved to be the most safe, speedy and certain cure for every species of Ague, and may be had of W. Lee, Jun. Bookseller, at Lewes, Price Five Shillings the Bottle.

• (W Lee being William, proprietor and editor of the *Sussex Weekly News.*)

This is another, purportedly a letter, of October 9, 1797:

I return you my sincere thanks for the great cure you have performed on me. I was afflicted with the scurvy and dropsy, likewise the yellow jaundice; my legs and body were swelled to an amazing manner; and at last it fell on my lungs, so that I could hardly breathe; I thought every moment would be my last; I tried many remedies, but all to no purpose, and everybody thought I could not live many days; but by the blessing of God, Dr.

Brodum, by his skill, and Botanical Syrup, made a perfect cure of me in a short time, which I am ready to attest on oath, either personally or by letter. Witness my hand,

Thomas Tobitt, Miller, at Mr Stovill's Mill, Steyning, Sussex.

Advertisement nailed to a tree near Horsham, 1779

Shaving's Dun here for a Penny Each
Pursson, Likewise Children carefully
Edicated in Reading, Righting,
And Account at this House by me

Notice on a signpost near Crowborough, 1787

This is to give notis to all gentelman farmers and millars, that the Cloube at Croborough Crope will contana as usal and to be 24 of this month September being Monday before the full moon and if the moon be at full on Monday 'tis to be on that day to meat 3 cloake The faver of thear company will mich oblight.

Even sillier

A man knocked on the door of a house and said he was collecting for Ringmer Swimming Pool. He was given a bucket of water.

When the people of Barcombe want to make a cart, they make a waggon and saw it in half.

Popular with visitors since 1066.
Hastings publicity slogan

Council speak

In Arun District Council's annual report of 1985, the chief executive, John Midgley, wrote:

> Local government is dominated at the present time by three key features that obligate recognition and response – societal change, resource management, political and customer accountability. Societal change arises from the impact and interaction of demographic, technological, economic, political, institutional and cultural factors. The scale, complexity and uncertainty of this change is immense. But it is the norm of existence nowadays creating vast problems for the nation and individual communities. Attention thereto requires high perception and perspective in order to achieve understanding the development of a coherent response strategy.

Or, as Bob Dylan put it: 'The times, they are a' changing'.

In 1985 Wealden District Council bought a 'plain-speaking computer' which required staff to re-learn the English language. Until then the officers had baffled the public, the press and their own elected members with an impenetrable language, probably learned in some secret establishment deep in the bosky weald, where it was passed on to new recruits by ancient mandarins who had selflessly spent their lives honing the secret communication system to perfection. But the Factors Affecting the Matter, as officers were wont to say, were that officers had to give up the obscure language and coding system that would baffle the brainpower of Bletchley. Details of the changeover were contained in a document referenced Constitution, Membership and Representation; Agendas, Reports, Minutes; Minutes; 85C/06PD Item 07(1): AC8001.8502b; (ADM/R5:Mins?TWD/1). This comprised twenty-six incomprehensibly numbered paragraphs meaty with tautology and jargon.

Norman Baker MP remained a parish councillor for Glynde and Beddingham until well after his election to Parliament, retiring only in May 2003. There was a legal requirement for separate annual meetings for each parish even though they operated together, he remembered:

> In the late '80s and early '90s the parish council used to meet in the schoolroom in Glynde, but this obviously did not meet the requirement for an annual meeting to be held in Beddingham. The contents of the annual meeting in Beddingham were virtually identical to those at Glynde and therefore a matter of going through the motions ... It did however seem a waste to use parish council funds to book a room for a very short meeting ... I well remember therefore on more than one occasion having the annual parish meeting on the pavement outside the Reading Room when the council would assemble and duly go through the agenda in record time before repairing to the pub.

Regency romps

Brighton's quite bizarre Royal Pavilion – which, to natives who've known it all their lives, is in no way extraordinary – was begun by Prince George (who became the Prince Regent and then George IV) in 1784 as his seaside residence, and completed in 1818. Of it, William Cobbett memorably wrote, in *Rural Rides*:

> The Kremlin, the very name of which has so long been a subject of laughter all over the country, lies in the gorge of the valley and amongst the old houses of the town. . . . when you see the thing from a distance, you think you see a parcel of cradle-spits, of various dimensions, sticking up out of the mouths of so many enormous squat decanters. Take a square box, the sides of which are three feet and a half, and the height of a foot and a half. Take a large Norfolk turnip, cut off the green of the leaves, leave the stalks nine inches long, tie these round with a string three inches from the top, and put the turnip on the middle of the top of the box. Then take four turnips of half the size, treat them in the same way, and put them on the corners of the box. Then take a considerable number of bulbs of the crown-imperial, the narcissus, the hyacinth, the tulip, the crocus, and others; let the leaves of each have sprouted to about an inch, more or less according to the size of the bulb; put all these, pretty promiscuously, but pretty thickly, on the top of the box. Then

'Turnips, bulbs and church-looking windows'

stand off and look at your architecture. There! That's a Kremlin! Only you must cut some church-looking windows in the sides of the box.

Charles Harper, author of *The Brighton Road*, thought it a tawdry, architectural enormity, the product of 'ill-informed enthusiasm for Chinese architecture, mingled with that of India and Constantinople'. It has also been described as 'architecturally contemptible' and 'a tasteless monstrosity'.

And one of the jolly songs in Noel Coward's *Conversation Piece* of 1934, where the action occurs in Regency Brighton, contains the following:

> The Pavilion
> Cost a million
> As monument to Art.
> And the wits here
> Say it sits here
> Like an Oriental tart.

The finger is pointed at Sidney Smith as the perpetrator of the most famous Pavilion insult: 'One would think that St Paul's Cathedral had come to Brighton and pupped'.

Practical joking was elevated to the status of a fine art at Brighton by the Prince and his merry men, according to Harper. A story is told of a drive to Brighton races, when the Prince was accompanied in his great yellow barouche by Townsend, the Bow Street runner, who was there to protect the Prince from insult or robbery at the hands of the multitude.

Turning suddenly to Townsend ... the Prince exclaimed, 'By Jove, Townsend, I've been robbed; I had with me some damson tarts, but they are now gone.' 'Gone!' said Townsend, rising. 'Impossible!' 'Yes,' rejoined the Prince, 'and you are the purloiner,' – at the same time taking from the seat whereon the officer had been sitting the crushed crust of the assorted missing tarts. The Prince added: 'This is a sad blot upon your reputation as a vigilant officer.' 'Rather say, your Royal Highness, a sad stain upon my escutcheon,' added Townsend, raising the gilt-buttoned tails of his blue coat and exhibiting the fruit-stained seat of his nankeen inexpressibles.

Admiral Sir Edmund Nagle, commander of the Brighton Sea Fencibles, was known to be very envious of the Prince's glorious pale Hanoverian horses and so was delighted to be presented with what he imagined was a horse from the Royal stud. Then it rained, and the admiral discovered that the animal was his own piebald horse, daubed with white paint.

A curious circumstance occurred at Brighton yesterday. Sir John Lade, for a trifling wager, undertook to carry Lord John Cholmondeley on his back from opposite the Pavilion twice round the Steine. Several ladies attended to be spectators of this extraordinary feat of the dwarf carrying the giant. When Lord Cholmondeley declared himself to be ready to be carried pick-a-back, Sir John Lade – who was a persistent wagerer – told him to strip. 'Strip! exclaimed the peer. 'Why, you promised to carry me in clothes.' 'Not so,' replied Sir John. 'I engaged, it is true, to carry you, not an inch of clothes, so, my lord, make ready.' Lord Cholmondeley declined to appear in the altogether and, after much laughable altercation, Sir John Lade was held to have won his bet. (*The Times*,1795)

Sir John won most of his wagers, but one he lost was to the Duke of Queensbury, who backed a notorious glutton to demolish 'more than could be eaten at a sitting' by a nominee of Sir John's. The stake was £1,000. The duke was later informed that his man 'beat his antagonist by a pig and an apple pie'.

Sir Edmund – the admiral – an habitué of the Old Ship Hotel's dining room, had a sharp wit of his own. When he read in *The Times* that 'Brighton fishermen, armed with swords and pikes, could be transformed into a formidable flotilla on the first appearance of danger', he is said to have countered that Brighton hoteliers, armed with their *bills*, would have scattered the enemy with their first *charge*.

A poor man near Brighton grew a huge turnip and sent it to the King (William IV, then in residence at the Pavilion) The King graciously accepted it and sent the man a guinea. Hearing this an individual bought and sent King William a beautiful, valuable horse. The King accepted, and immediately sent the huge turnip in return, saying the horse was so fine that he must give something equally fine of its kind. The man was not pleased.

Nigel Richardson (a 'furriner' but one who knows us better than we know ourselves, so we'll probably have to adopt him), in his 1998 book *Breakfast in Brighton*, uses a mere handful of words to describe the magical metamorphosis that transformed a poverty-stricken, bad-smelling village into a the world's smartest, most extravagant holiday resort.

> In the eighteenth century Brighton was still a fishing hamlet with snub nose, freckles and an awkward name: Brighthelmstone. One night the seagulls went to sleep and when they woke up their little town was cool and knowing, ingeniously sexy. Norma Jean Baker became Marilyn Monroe. It was one of history's greatest makeovers.

Brighton's splendid seafront of grand mansions – the seaside homes of George's court – was (and is still in some places) sometimes a facade, and the reason is bungaroush. While the fronts of some houses in the terraces, squares and crescents were fashioned from sturdy stone, the rest was often of this stuff called bungaroush – a mixture of lime, flint, beach pebbles, bits of this and bits of that. What used to be called 'Queen Anne front, Mary Ann back'.

> Bungaroush became synonymous with shoddy worksmanship, as if the property speculators and builders of Regency times were jerrybuilders and fly-by-nights who whacked up these apparently grand edifices any old which way. Bungaroush was a very Brightonian concept. The word sounded dashing but bogus, an ostler from Patcham masquerading as a Levantine prince. (Richardson, again)

Today's restorers and renovators complain that when drilled into, the flints and pebbles spin and shift and walls, apparently, can crumble to a pile of dusty debris – yet all of these grand buildings remain standing today. A triumph for dashing, bogus bungaroush.

Thirty days hath September,
April, June and no wonder.
Everybody likes strawberry jam,
Except my grandmother,
Who rides a bicycle.

From a 1950s Brighton rag mag

From bad to verse

There are as many comic epitaphs, daft limericks and awful odes of, by and about the people of Sussex (and their county) as elsewhere. Here are a few:

The funnier epitaphs are perhaps the most suspect – for instance this one was supposed to have been spotted in Storrington churchyard, but nobody has yet seen it:

Here lies the body of Edward Hide,
We laid him here because he died.
We had rather,
It had been his father.
If it had been his sister,
We should have missed her.
But since 'tis honest Ned,
No more shall be said.

Little Jack Horner sat in a corner
Outrage had rendered him dumb.
His mood had been soured by
what he'd devoured:
A genetically modified plum!

By Paul Weston of Brighton, quoted in the *Daily Mail's* Peterborough

The next was written by William Lee, newspaper proprietor and entrepreneur, for the grave of an illiterate horse-dealer of Lewes, a Mr Drowley:

Here lies a man that lived by lying.
Some people thought 'twould leave him dying.
But to the nation's great surprise,
Even in his grave he lies.

The following was said to have 'graced a grave in a Downland churchyard':

Here lies the Mother of children seven.
Three on earth, and four in heaven.
The four in heaven preferring rather,
To be with Mother, than live with Father.

And can we really believe in this one?:

Here lies daughter Charlotte,
Who was born a virgin, and died a harlot.
For fifteen years she kept her virginity,
Not a bad record for this vicinity.

This is from *The Book of Wisdom,* an eighteenth century manuscript written by William Wisdom of Glynde, edited by Andrew Lusted. Wisdom saw what he described as an 'Epitaph on a Person who had lately kept a Shop of Brown Earthenware' in 1776, hanging in a room 'at old Mr Richard Mocket's, Gibralter, Firle. He told me himself and Glover Ansell won it at the Swan in the Cliff, Lewes. The terms were if you made it out you had it for nothing. If you attempted but could not do it you paid a pot.'

> Ben Eathth is s Tone Li Es cath Erine g Ray ch Ang dfr Om ab Usy Li Fe t O li Fe Les Scl
> Ay B Ye Ar Th A nDcl Ays heg Ot He Rs Elf Ye We EP ing fr IEN dS le Tm Ea Dvi SE –
> AB Atey Ourg Ri Ef ANd wiPe YO urE yES Fo Rwh At aVa ILSA FL OODOF TEA R S
> Wh OkN OwSBU tina Ru NO FY eARS I nsOm TAll pi tCh ERORTA 11 p An Sh Ein he
> RS HOP M A yc O ME AGAIN

The *Sussex County Magazine* of revered memory (born 1927, died 1956) was unequalled on local history and landscape photography, but was terribly addicted to publishing vile verse by genteel ladies who, from all appearances, believed in 'pharisees' (fairies).

> *They dewponds on the Downland*
> *Why is't them holds the dew?*
> *Sure Pharisees dance round 'em:*
> *Aye, and they bathe there, too.*

Tain't Bookses hold such knowledge
That ain't for folks in Towns
We Shepherds don't know College,
But sure we know these Downs!

A Bosham butcher received this Valentine in 1950 (when there was post-war rationing, still):

Will you, darling butcher mine,
Be my loving Valentine?
Failing that, I'll gladly take
A little extra stewing steak.
Will you, butcher, dearest dear,
Be my Valentine this year?
Failing that, perhaps you'd sneak
Me some extra chops this week.
Will you, though you've got a wife,
Be my Valentine for life?
Failing that, my handsome prince,
Could I have a little mince?

Now We Are Sick

Hush, Hush,
Nobody cares!
Christopher Robin
Has
Fallen
Down
Stairs.

This is J B Morton's take on A A Milne's *Now We Are Six*. Morton, the original Beachcomber columnist, lived in Rodmell.

And here are a few amusing limericks

A gardener out at Hurst Green
Grew a marvellous kind of French bean:
The judge at the show
Said: 'I really don't know
Where a Frencher French bean can be seen.

A musician who lived at Hoathly
All rules of his art would defy:
And cacophones wrote
Upon which he would dote,
'Til his neighbours compelled him to fly.

A forgetful old scholar of Lavant
When asked for his name said: 'I haven't
The slightest idea
What I'm called: ain't it queer?
But I know I'm a very good savant.

There was an old cleric of Rottingdean
Who said: 'I'm no longer a swotting dean.
I am taking my ease
And I'm growing sweat peas,
I'm a hoeing and sowing and potting dean.'

An eccentric old person of Brighton
To a very long string tied a kite on.
The kite wouldn't rise
It was too great a size
So he dragged it along with a light on

*In 1933, a Major
Weston – disgusted of
Bethersden – appalled
at the desecration
wrought at hitherto
untouched beauty
spots (especially at
High and Over
between Alfriston and
Seaford) by the new
car-owning
'townsmen', wrote to
the Sussex County
Magazine of his
'horror and disgust'at
this invasion; 'The
Mark of the Beast', he
called it.*

In trade

William Wisdom wrote, in 1811:

Philip Lyon, the Jew, kept a very decent shop near the Bear Inn in the Cliff and went often to the barracks at the foot of Lewes Hill with his box, calling on Mr. William's Pelham Arms for a glass of refreshment. Mr Williams ... was very inquisitive to know what he went there for. Philip told him it was to sell them flea powder. Mr. W wished to have a shillingsworth, which Lyon brought him the next day and received the cash for. But, just as he was going, Mr. W said 'You must tell me how I am to use it'. 'Oh, said Philip, 'you must catch them first and give dem a d----d hard pinch on de back which will make dem open their mouths den clap in a little of de powder and it will kill dem directly.'

Around the same year the young Ellman was living with his parents in Southover Manor, Lewes, and he remembered a visit from the flea powder man. Philip (for it must have been he) had a ready answer for customers who complained, Ellman wrote:

> Thus if a person told him that if he could catch a flea he would not want the powder to kill it, he would civilly say, 'Of course, sir, you can kill it what way you like'; or if told that the powder was of no use, he would say, 'How could you expect the powder to have any effect unless you made the flea take it?'

Marcus Woodward told the following, attributing it to Baring Gould.

> A Sussex butcher, after marrying a wife and carrying her off on a honeymoon, insisted, to her vast surprise and indignation, on weighing her upon his shop's meat-scales. His earnest desire was to enter the expenses of the honeymoon in his account-book. To work these out on a scale he could understand he had decided to divide the costs of the honeymoon by the weight of his wife. Making a calculation, he muttered, in a way showing he was not best pleased at what the scale told him: 'Cost me fourteen pence ha'penny a pound: the dearest bit of meat that ever I bought!'

Bill presented to Sussex farmer in 1861 by the village carpenter:

> To hanging two barn doors and myself 7 hours, four shillings and 6d.

Flights of fancy

World-class silliness may be seen at Bognor every August (or June, it being a moveable feast, depending on the tide) when

Eastbourne Herald

Chichester Observer

around 30 lunatics, watched by 40,000 spectators, throw themselves off the end of Bognor Pier in an assortment of loony flying craft, or with just a superhero-style cape to give a lift.

The record for the longest flight , set in 1992 by David Bradshaw, is 89.2m. Competitors, who come from all over Britain – and all over the world, too – then move on to Eastbourne Pier to have another go.

In the top picture is The Flying Frogman (Ed Simpson), a 2002 competitor at Bognor. Below left is an aerodynamically-challenged Eastbourne 2003 entrant.

Pudding

'Don't go to Sussex or they'll turn you into a pudding,' outsiders used to be told. Sussex housewives turned just about everything into puddings – meat, fruit, vegetables, fish, poultry, even weeds and flowers. They made puddings in ball or sausage shapes, wrapped them tightly in cloths and plunged them into a large pot of boiling water (or sometimes the copper where the weekly wash was done, which must have added a weirdly soapy flavour). Generally puddings were made with suet and flour, but in poor households they did without the suet, and mixed flour, water and a pinch of salt to make a 'hard dick' – a pudding containing nothing. Before it was cooked in boiling water, the pudding was put aside to 'set'. William Parish blamed hard dick, when eaten cold, for 'all the ills the flesh is heir to':

> It aggravates every natural infirmity of temper by the promotion of chronic indigestion, and finally undermines the constitution. The first symptom of the decay of nature which a Sussex man describes is invariably that he can't get his pudding to set.

A glutinous grey mess called plumb pudding was a peculiar Sussex dish that was eaten as a starter, a between-course appetiser and often a finisher too. Typically it consisted of a leg or shin or beef, six penny loaves, five pounds of currants, five pounds of raisins, two pounds of prunes, spices, three pounds of sugar, two pints of claret, lemons and sago – all of which was cooked for hours and hours until it became a sort of thick gruel that resembled stone building material when cold. Around Christmas-time in 1796 a Cuckfield flax dresser wagered he could eat a square foot of plumb pudding, weighing 42lb, in a fortnight. The *Sussex Weekly Advertiser*, a newspaper that knew a good human interest story when it saw one, sent along a reporter who recorded the events for posterity.

January 9, 1797: The man who undertook to eat his way through 2 lbs more than a moiety of it on Wednesday last which was his seventh day's performance, ate 4 lbs at his first meal, but appeared rather crop-sick for the remainder of the day and the next. By way of science, he sometimes uses a great quantity of mustard with his pudding, and at other times, sops it with vinegar.

January 16: The plum-pudding eater on the eighth day found his gormandizers jaws absolutely refusing to stir any longer in the service; in consequence of which he was reluctantly necessitated to give in.

Our food is freshly prepared so please bare with us at busy times.

Menu displayed at the Nag's Head, Chichester

Coarse, uninviting food was known in Sussex as 'the sirloin of a jackass, stuffed with sodgers', sodger being a soldier.

Animal crackers

Philip Gosse, in *Go to the Country*, wrote of a childhood holiday on a farm near Pulborough:

The farmer was named Smale. My father was always muddling up the name of the dog, Smart, with that of his master, which was apt sometimes to lead to odd misunderstandings, as when my father protested to Mrs. Smale saying, 'You really must not allow Smale to come into our part of the house, he has just been sick again on the carpet.'

The Gosse family took their pets with them on holiday.

There was Lady Port, the guinea pig, wife of, or anyhow the mother of the children of, Lord Bacon. I do not suppose I would remember Lady Pork at all after all these years were it not for something which happened at her funeral. I cannot even remember what she died of, nor if her last illness was long or short, nor if her end was a peaceful one. But I do remember very clearly her funeral. A pathetically small grave was dug in the apple orchard. The mourners consisted of my father and mother, my two sisters, myself, Lord Bacon, and the deceased's own particular friend, Smart, the farmer's sheep-dog. Smart, being the chief mourner, walked at the head of the slow-moving cortege. After the little coffin had been lowered into the grave, the earth replaced and flowers scattered over the tiny mound, and a small cross erected with this simple inscription: 'LADY PORT We will never forget you', the mourners returned sadly and silently to the house. None of us children felt inclined for play, our thoughts were with the dear departed. Then while we sat listlessly about one of my sisters suddenly said, 'I wonder where Smart is'. In such sad circumstances any excuse is good enough to distract the thoughts of the bereaved, and a search was begun for the missing mourner. At last he was found He had returned to the orchard, to the newly made grave, and when discovered was in the act of consuming the last portion of his little friend.

A little booklet, bound in cardboard and called *The Tale of a Crab: A Rigmarole*, was published in Sussex around 1820. An anonymous satire or a lampoon, it had nineteen pages of humorous drawings illustrating the tale of a fisherwoman who was crossing the Downs with a basket of fish (presumably along Juggs Road from Brighton) when, unobserved by her, a live crab escaped from her basket. The crab was discovered by a shepherd who has never seen so strange a beast and fled at its approach, rushing down the hill into the village (could it be Kingston?).

The villagers armed themselves with pitchforks and set forth to attack the creature but when they saw the fearsome monster they were so frightened they turned tail and ran. The oldest inhabitant was consulted. He asked to see the beast and was conveyed in a wheelbarrow up the hill to the spot where the crab was last seen. He clapped eyes on the crustacean and declared it to be a 'spread eagle' or a 'Roman Catholic' or a 'wild Irishman'. Finally, after much consideration, he decided it was, in fact, a Roman Catholic.

A couple of hundred years ago the eleventh Duke of Norfolk introduced a colony of owls to his castle at Arundel. Over the years the birds bred and multiplied and were given grand names after leading figures of the age and friends of the noble family. The most celebrated of the owls was Lord Thurlow. At a gathering of lords and ladies one day a castle emissary rushed in and announced: 'Please, your Grace, the Lord Thurlow has laid an egg!' It is said that the owl, which kept its name despite the egg, lived on until 1859 when it was reputedly a centenarian.

An old grey mare, leading horse in the Bognor voluntary fire brigade's dash to a blaze at Yapton one evening a century ago, reached the scene of the fire, collapsed and died from the exertion. 'Well I'm danged,' said her fireman owner. 'I've never known the old grey mare do that before.' A true story, it is claimed.

A wandering ventriloquist proved such a hit when he entertained drinkers at the Crown Inn in Hailsham that nineteenth-century local toff Richard King-Sampson invited the man to breakfast with him the next morning. According to Thomas Geering: 'The meal over, he was taken to the stables. The groom, an elderly man in blue gaberdine, was in attendance. The stranger stood in the stall, patting and praising the favourite hunter, speaking well of the glossy coat, and tickling the groom's conceit, when the master asked, "Have you fed him this morning, George?" "Yes, sir" – with a nasal twang – was the reply. "No, you have not,' gloomily and very deliberately said the horse. "What!" said George; "tell you I have." "No, you have not," emphasized the horse. "What do you mean?" said George, "tell you I have." "No, you have not,"said the horse again. "And what do you mean, George?" said his master. "The horse says plainly you have not fed him." "Tell you I have," again said George. "Tell you you have not." The dispute was running high, when the wizard, opening the mouth of the animal, said, "How old are you?" "Seven," said the sleek hunter. This was too much for the old groom who, rushing out of the stable, declared the devil must be in the place; and much did his master enjoy the chagrin of the poor old man. He was soon recalled and reasoned with, but George always declared that the horse did talk. He could never settle in his mind any other way. "'Twas done so naa-tur-el," he said. "But he lied though; I had fed him.'"

In the days before car ferries from Newhaven, when the railway company ran a passenger service, a hugely valuable prize cat arrived from London for despatch to a new home in Paris. The night shift, feeling sorry for the cat, took it from the basket to give it a bite to eat. The cat escaped into the East Side allotments where gangs of wild cats roamed. Railway staff searched high and low throughout the night, without success. But a wild cat was captured, placed in the basket and sent off to Paris. What happened next? Nothing was ever heard

Property section

New things are generally old. Take the pre-fab, for instance. Not, as you may imagine, a post-Second World War temporary dwelling for homeless returning heroes, or even a nasty sixties concrete tower block. No. The pre-fab is one thousand years old, and it first appeared in Sussex.

William the Conqueror, certain of success when he waded ashore in 1066, wanted a castle ready for immediate occupation after his victory. Back in Normandy he'd had a sectional wooden building constructed, secured by bolts for rapid dis-assembly and re-assembly. The castle parts were shipped over with the invading force, and off went William to meet Harold in battle – meanwhile ordering his carpenters to set up the castle on a nice spot with a sea view.

So quickly was it erected that, according to a jokey local legend, the site of the world's first pre-fab was given the name of Hastings. (Actually, the name comes from the Haestingas, a northern European tribe that settled the area).

Gerard Young wrote in *The Cottage in the Fields*:

England's first pre-fab

Sussex has seen much in the way of settlement since the arrival of the English from across the North Sea. A later invasion came from inland and in the last decade of the nineteenth century. The invaders, bringing with them their own dialects and customs, settled chiefly on the coast, or more precisely, on the very beach itself and erected their bizarre dwellings mainly of wood and bearing a striking affinity to butchered railway carriages. This new English settlement was flourishing by 1919 and, closely following the water line, it spread rapidly east and west from the mother township south of Shoreham which became presently identified on the map as Bungalow Town, from the Hindu-Saxon *bangala-tun*.

Infiltrating swiftly among the older British settlements and encountering little but 'Letter-to-the-Editor' opposition, the neo-English invasion in a short space of time had reached Brighton, seized and transformed Rottingdean, advanced through Bexhill to Hastings and spread rapdily towards the Kent border. Similarly westwards the hitherto lonely sand-dunes of Lancing vanished beneath the crop of discarded S.R. rolling stock and corrugated iron. Marshlands to the east of Worthing caused a slight inland colonisation, but it was not

Bungalow town home created from an old railway carriage, wrecked by a storm in 1912

long before the invaders had by-passed the town and reached the sea again at Goring preparatory to the great drive westwards in the late 1920s and early 1930s.

Apropos Lancing and strange buildings, a great-aunt once lived in Old Salts Farm Road, then a very rough track. The potholes were immense; an inept child falling into one would find herself waist-deep in muddy water that seemed to remain all year long.

Aunty lived with her unmarried adult children in a magical place that began as a First World War medical hut. Over time additions appeared: a punkah wallahish verandah on the

Bricks in the mouth and on the net

A Sussex estate agent employs a copy-writer with a quaint turn of phrase. He/she wrote of a 'desirable and chique' cottage, a country house with 'a cultured garden' and a home that's 'intrigue and character still hang onto echoes of the past'.

The company's 'Spanish desk' (a huge, heavily carved mahogany job maybe) is 'supported on a network of contacts', where legs may have been preferable.

Those who fly out to Spain to inspect properties are met by an 'English-speaking agent' who perhaps would be better employed in the home office.

The London office is said to 'draw like a magnet many high quality cash rich clients, many letting their homes in London seeking properties in the south'.

And this – 'when a new property enters the market it will be emailed to you at the touch of a button' – could bring the web crashing down under a ton or six of

front; suites of rooms for the children (and their lovers – Aunty was very *avant garde* for the 1940s) on the sides; a grand 'Georgian' drawing room on the back. The original hut, which was really quite spacious, became a central, timbered 'baronial' hall. A true eccentric, Aunty knitted a large turquoise rug for this hall. When it became dirty, she hauled it into the bath and turned on the taps, but the rug was so big it could be neither washed nor removed, and there it stayed for many months. So much classier than the traditional coal.

'Well-presented two-bedroom detached bungalow. Separate wc and driveway.'
Seen in Adnews, Hastings

Despite her great age (well, it seemed great, but probably she was no more than early sixties) Aunty was keen on nice young sailors and regretted she couldn't see their passing ships from her single-storey home. So she had stairs constructed and two rooms built in the roof space. One was above the drawing room and contained massive, ormolu-mounted cupboardry and a great marble table that was never used (so far as anyone knew) for any purpose other than the laying-out of her estranged husband (who had lived nearby with his mistress but returned home for the occasion), and the second was a smallish bedroom equipped with a porthole and a telescope for spying on the sailors at sea.

Aunty had what was said to be a Louis XIV four-poster which, naturally, did not fit into this new small bedroom, so a man came to saw it down the middle and reduce the post height. Re-erected upstairs, the thin, squat four-poster was surrounded by newspaper on which Aunty's plants benefited from rainwater coming through the leaky roof.

A boring block of flats now occupies the site of Aunty's magical house.

Reportedly

Newspaper journalists used to copy down the names on the wreaths at funerals to list in their reports, and when rival reporters from different papers were present they helped each other out by doing it between them. At one funeral in the 1950s a reporter, whom we may call Arthur, refused to help men from two other local papers because his editor no longer published such details. Arthur, who happened to be very drunk, fell into the open grave, and the other two declined to help him out. Eventually he was rescued by the undertakers' men just as the coffin was being borne from the church. Arthur met his end when, wending his way home after a glass or two one day, he was run over by a milk float and died.

At another funeral, Arthur's colleague, Douglas, was standing at the church door after the service, asking mourners for their names. Out came a tall, distinguished man. 'Excuse me, sir, may I have your name?' said Douglas. 'It's Harold Macmillan,' said the good-humoured Prime Minister of the day. 'That's capital M, a, c, small m, i double l, a n.'

Helpful Premier

Whoever said reporters had to know anything? Those moving from 'meeja college' to trainee jobs on local papers today are sometimes quite spectacularly clueless. A young Sussex-born and -bred person, whom we

Colourfully

Famous Brighton Back Passages.
Brighton Festival event in 2002

He took his part in both hands, extracted the utmost from it and reached his climax without once losing control.
Lewes Little Theatre review

You will find the best selection of Bridesmaids, available in almost any colour you could wish for.'

may call Billy, inherited from his sons-of-the-soil ancestors all the daft-old-gitness about which toffs used to scoff. Billy (aged twenty-two) was always asking questions – which was no bad thing in a reporter. 'Trombola – it's a music thing, isn't it?' 'Is Mongolia a country or a district?' 'Do dogs have hooves?' 'Is the Andes a mountain?'

Billy on the phone: 'Sealion? Sealon? What's that then, a sort of sea animal? Can you spell it? c e y l o n. What's a ceylon? Oh I see. It's a country. But it's not called that any more. So what's it called now? What? Sreelanker? Can you spell that please? So where is this country?'

Billy typed: 'They enjoyed a slap-up three course meal'.

He asked a sub-editor: 'So how many people's a three course meal for?'

Sub: 'One.'

Billy: 'You sure?'

Required to write a Kipling-related story, Billy asked: 'So who's this Roodyard Kipling?'

Sub: 'You've heard of the cake-maker, Mr Kipling?'

Billy: 'Yeah.'

Sub: 'Rudyard was one of those Kiplings. In 1860 Lockwood Kipling went out to India to set up a cake factory, where he perfected the Poona Battenberg, but the climate was too hot and the cakes disintegrated in their cellophane wrappings. So he packed the entire factory on a dromedary train and set off for the hills where the climate would be more equable.'

Billy, taking notes: 'Yeah?'

Sub: 'Yeah. Rudyard Kipling was Lockwood's younger brother. The family sent him out to India to help with the cake factory, but he was useless at business and took instead to writing stories and poems.'

Billy: 'Yeah?'

Sub: 'Yeah.'

Billy: 'So yeah. This dromedary train? Was it like early steam or something?'

Last Saturday a Journeyman Carpenter at Brighton, who suspected his wife of being too familiar with one of the Band belonging to the Derbyshire Militia, resolved on satisfying his doubts; he accordingly put on his best suit, and after taking leave of his rib, set out on his pretended journey. Her sparkling eyes flashed joy at his departure, and she soon communicated the happy circumstance to her beloved Orpheus, who lost no time in stringing his lyre, and charming her with the force of his tunes; but sad to tell, the husband unexpectedly returned and interrupted the unison, just as it was vibrating its sweetest chords, and so belaboured poor Orpheus, that it is thought he will never attempt to play the second part of the same tune.
Sussex Weekly Advertiser, May 18, 1798

Reporting on a successful August Bank Holiday, the *Worthing Gazette* said the hotels had been full, the weather fine, the beaches packed – but there had been complaints from residents about 'couples making love in pubic places'.

A Sussex book, 'recommended for the closet', is the exhaustively entitled 1698 tome, *A Compleat History of the Most Remarkable Providences, Both of Judgment and Mercy, Which have Hapned in this Present Age. Extracted from the Best Writers, the Author's own Observations, and the Numerous Relations sent him from divers Parts of the Three Kingdoms. To which is Added, Whatever is Curious in the Works of Nature and Art. The Whole Digested into One Volume, under Proper Heads; being a Work set on Foot Thirty Years ago, by the Reverend Mr. Poole, Author of the Synopsis Criticorum: and since Undertaken and Finished, By William Turner, M.A., Vicar of Walberton, in Sussex. Recommended as useful to Ministers in Furnishing Topicks of Reproof and Exhortation, and to Private Christians for their Closets and Families.*

No need to read it then, the title having said it all. It was printed by book seller John Raven 'at the Raven, in Jewen-Street, MDCXCVII'.

Toe Nail Chippings, eight-year collection. First to see will buy. Jar of fond memories. £1.

Advertisement in Friday-Ad

This was written by a newspaper advertising salesman who was unable to persuade any of the journalists with whom he worked to go for a free meal and write a 'puff' about a restaurant – so decided to do it himself. But how many journalists can sell ads?

Unlike many other adventures to new and unfamiliar civilisations unable to be revisited, the vain of authenticity lends itself to the ambience that ensues.

A Hove artist described his work thus in a press release:

The surface effects from the light and colour surrounding the architecture. Since, the fusion of new and old architecture is very important to the theme; it makes sense that the ways, in which the pieces are constructed, echo this ... Alike classic archways and features of older buildings married with modern metallic constructions that can be found with office blocks and other modern buildings.

Womens' Institute press correspondents can be entertaining.

'Mrs A was excellent, both boiled and unboiled. This was much enjoyed.'

'We had a display of knitted tarts.'

Barbed wire toilet seat, never used.

Advertisement in Friday Ad

'And finally I should like to wish all readers who are getting married in the near future every health and happiness. Good luck, both of you.'

Gallimaufry

This is the Great Omi, whose entire body was tattoed zebra-style. He had a double-pointed tusk through his nose and ivory daggers and rings through his ears. Horace Riddler was an army officer who squandered an inheritance, failed at various jobs and became a drifter before deciding to turn himself into a freak – 'The World's Strangest Human Being' – in order to make a living. He and his wife, Omette, lived in a mobile home at Golden Cross. He died there in 1965.

Charles Yeates, in a little booklet called *Laughter is Free* (undated, but probably around 1970) wrote of his childhood friend, Tommy, in the early years of twentieth century in Brighton. The family was poor, and Tommy's father would have a bloater, heated in a frying pan of water, for his dinner while Tommy had the bloater skin between two slices of bread for his. Yeates wrote:

His poor old mother would stand at our street door with my mother, both of them in starched white aprons that reached down to their ankles, gossiping and chiding passers-by. I certainly will not name the old darling, but she was nearly crippled with her feet dreadfully distorted by bunions and rheumatism. About a mile away, out on the hill on the outskirts of the town, was the Borough Cemetery, and from our doorstep could be seen the acres of marble tombstones shining in the sunlight. And Tommy's mother would stand there complaining and cringing with the pain of her poor feet and I heard her once say to my mother: 'Look up there Nell. Hundreds of brand new bleedin' feet being buried every week, and I'm stuck here with these buggers!'

Austin Shorney wrote of driving home to East Grinstead in his 'decrepit old car':

A really thick freezing fog closed the night in and I had a difficult time driving home at little more than a walking pace, with no heater and with my head out of the window half the time. By the time I reached The White Hart at

Sticky business

Sussex is rich in treacle mines – at Rowhook, Polegate, Faygate, Sompting and Lewes, evidently.

The mine at Faygate even had its own docks – at Rusper. And Sompting Treacle Mine had its history documented by Alfred Longley in *Alexandra Terrace*.

The chimney at Sompting could be lowered to allow the harvest moon to pass without getting stuck to it.

Lewes Treacle Mine's entrance was through double doors in the cliff at Offham.

Ardingly I was more than ready for a little comfort, so I went in for a whisky. At the bar were a couple of farm workers and a man with a parrot on his shoulder. The bird was having frequent sips of whisky from his owner's glass and I watched out of reddened eyes, fascinated. 'Would you like to see him stand on his head?' asked the bird's owner. 'Indeed I would,' I said. Whereupon he smoothed down the bird's wings several times, held out his palm and placed the bird in it where it remained, upside down, wings folded and quite rigid for a full thirty seconds. This called for more whisky all round. Out I went to a freezing car to battle with the fog again. When at last I reached home, Ruby opened the door and I said: 'I've just seen a parrot, standing on its head!' She gave one sniff. 'You're drunk!' she said. I was rather too tired to explain.

High tea

Teapot feature on a Peacehaven roof. Why? And how?

Lilian Candlin recalled, in *Memories of Old Sussex*:

A member of Coolham WI told me a few years ago about a health visitor in the Chichester area. One day she had to call at a house about a bed-wetting case. The father opened the door and told her that she need not call any more as they had tried his grandmother's cure and the child was now quite cured. When the health visitor asked him what the remedy was, he replied, 'We boiled a mouse in milk and gave it to the child to drink.'

Newhaven's Eastside is known as Turkey Town. Why? The story is that one December, some time in the 1920s, a ship arrived at the East Quay carrying a cargo of live, plump turkeys from Normandy. They were destined for the Christmas tables of grand families and ritzy hotels. But something happened between the arrival of the ship and forwarding of the consignment by train. Suffice to say that while orders went unfulfilled because there were insufficient turkeys, the families of dock workers living in the cosy little Eastside community each had a whopping bird on the table that Christmas. Hence the dock area's nickname.

And by the way – there's this local joke: 'A bomb fell on Newhaven town centre and caused five million pounds' worth of improvement.'

Mice, evidently, were once a staple in the Sussex pharmacopoeia. Here's the well-known whooping cough and headache cure from the diary of Anthony Stapley (1657-1724) of Twineham:

Get three field mice; flaw them; draw them; and roast one of them, and let the afflicted

Marmaduke, a topiary mog seen on a wall in Eastport Lane, Lewes

party eat it. Dry the other two in the oven until they crumble to powder, and put a little of this powder in what the patient drinks at night, and in the morning.

And still with rodents – a Portslade doctor ordered a mother to tie a bag of ice to her feverish son's forehead. When he asked later how the boy was, the mother said he was much better, but the mice were all dead.

Even nastier than mice remedies, was what was said to be the only really efficient cure for glandular trouble in young women. Stroking a girl's neck with the hand of a man who had just been hanged did the trick, according to an old superstition. The 'death stroke' was also pretty good as a cure for wens.

Thomas Shoyswell, of Shoyswell Manor, Etchingham, left to his wife Dorothy in 1580 among other gifts: 'the cubberd that standeth at my bede head and the use and wering of her weddinge ring for lief.'

114

From the parish register:

Richard Bassett, the old clarke of this parish (Buxted), who had continued in the offices of clarke and sexton for the space of 43 years, whose melody warbled forth as if he had been thumped on the back with a stone, was buried the 20th of Sept. 1666.

Buried Thomas Winfield that old fornicator (Ashburnham 1576).

Baptised William, son of Anne Robarts by God Knows Who (Angmering 1765).

Baptised Harriet, base born daughter of Elizabeth Rogers, a very noted Strumpet of this Parish (Wadhurst 1784).

The sign for the Moonrakers Restaurant in Alfriston has two chaps standing in the Cuckmere river with rakes. Why? Legend says they were smugglers caught by the revenue men in the act of retrieving their booty from the water. What are you doing, the officers demanded. Why, we're raking up the moon, they replied with rustic guilelessness – and thereupon proceeded to rake at the moon's reflection in the water. True, it's said.

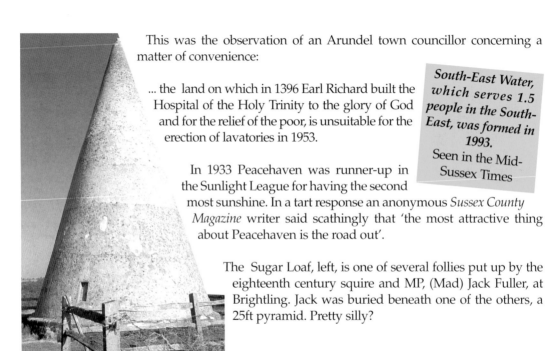

This was the observation of an Arundel town councillor concerning a matter of convenience:

... the land on which in 1396 Earl Richard built the Hospital of the Holy Trinity to the glory of God and for the relief of the poor, is unsuitable for the erection of lavatories in 1953.

South-East Water, which serves 1.5 people in the South-East, was formed in 1993.
Seen in the Mid-Sussex Times

In 1933 Peacehaven was runner-up in the Sunlight League for having the second most sunshine. In a tart response an anonymous *Sussex County Magazine* writer said scathingly that 'the most attractive thing about Peacehaven is the road out'.

The Sugar Loaf, left, is one of several follies put up by the eighteenth century squire and MP, (Mad) Jack Fuller, at Brightling. Jack was buried beneath one of the others, a 25ft pyramid. Pretty silly?

A Sussex hoax goes international

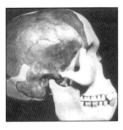

The Piltdown Man scam was one of the more enjoyable silly things of Sussex. In 1912 Uckfield lawyer and amateur archaeologist Charles Dawson 'found' what was declared the skull of Lower Pleistocene man, around 150,000 years old, in river gravel near Piltdown. Forty years later more accurate dating methods showed that the cranium belonged to the very much younger Upper Pleistocene man – while the jaw came from a modern ape and had been doctored to appear prehistoric. Meanwhile, discovery of the 'missing link' had captured the attention of leading scholars, archaeologists and geologists from around the globe. Many learned books and papers were penned over the years until science exposed the fraud in 1953. In the aftermath, *Sussex County Magazine* writer Francis Vere wrote (rather weirdly):

Whenever the name of our beloved County is mentioned nowadays – in Hong Kong with millions of Communists across the water, in Honduras with Revolution at the back door, or at some restaurant or club in the West End of London – someone will at once say: 'Ah! Piltdown is in Sussex, isn't it?' and – when you have coyly pleaded guilty – 'Ah! What a hoax that was!'

Select bibliography and sources

Armstrong, Anthony: *Village at War*
Blaker, Nathaniel Paine: *Sussex in Bygone Days*
Buckeridge, Anthony: *While I Remember*
Candlin, Lilian: *Memories of Old Sussex*
Ditchling History Project: *Memories of War*
Egremont, Lord: *Wyndham and Children First*
Ellman, Edward Boys: *Recollections of a Sussex Parson*
Gage, Lord: *Memories of Firle*
Geering, Thomas: *Our Parish*
Gosse, Philip: *Go to the Country*
Harper, Charles: *The Brighton Road*
Lucas, EV: *Highways and Byways in Sussex*
Lusted, Andrew, ed: *The Book of Wisom*
Moore, Judy: *Sampling Sussex*
Moore J, Voit, A: *Memories of Roedean*
Parish, WD: *The Dictionary of Sussex Dialect*
Pearson, John: *Stags and Serpents*

Richardson, Nigel: *Breakfast in Brighton*
Shorney, Austin: *Forget and Smile*
Thurston Hopkins, R: *Sussex Pilgrimages*
Trimingham, Adam: *Trimingham's Brighton*
Woodward, Marcus: *The Mistress of Stantons Farm*

Also: reminiscences of Doris M Hall and Edmund Austen; *Sussex County Magazine* and various county newspapers.

This collection barely scratches the surface of the rich mine of Sussex daftness. If any readers have suitable sillinesses for a follow-up book I will receive them gratefully and be happy to acknowledge your contributions. You may contact me on JEMeditorial@aol.com or via SB Publications at 19 Grove Road, Seaford, East Sussex, BN25 1TP.

Thanks are due to John Morris, Kevin Penfold and Brigid Chapman; to the *Sussex Express*, Gerry Thompson of New Age Eddie Cards (07905 417470) and *Chichester Observer*; to St Peter's School, Chailey, *Eastbourne Herald*, and to Mike Hemsley of Walter Gardiner Photography (01903 200528).

Delicious – the Brighton to Tunbridge Wells bus seen at Lewes bus station